THE SCARS OF THE MOON

SHORT STORIES

Kraftgriots

Also in the series (SHORT STORIES)

Asomwan Adagbonyin (ed.): *Frontiers*
Promise Onwudiwe: *Soul-Journey into the Night*
Chinyere Okafor: *He Wants to Marry Me Again and Other Stories*
Titi Ufomata: *Voices From the Marketplace*

THE SCARS OF THE MOON

SHORT STORIES

Isiaka Aliagan

Published by

Kraft Books Limited
6A Polytechnic Road, Sango, Ibadan
Box 22084, University of Ibadan Post Office
Ibadan, Oyo State, Nigeria
✆ 234 (02) 8106655
E-mail: krabooks@skannet.com

© Isiaka Aliagan 1999

First published 2000

ISBN 978–039–022–7

= KRAFTGRIOTS =
(A literary imprint of Kraft Books Limited)

All Rights Reserved

First printing, July 2000

Printmarks Ventures, Ososami, Ibadan.

For
Asiaw and **Nana Aisha**t,
wife and daughter

Acknowledgments

I wish to place on record the invaluable assistance of the former Military Administrator of Kwara State, Lt. Colonel Rashid Alade Shekoni (rtd) for the success of the compilation of these short stories.

I also benefited from the wisdom of friends and colleagues who went through the stories. I thank Dr. Saleh Abdu for writing the introduction and Femi Dunmade of the Department of Modern European Languages of the University of Ilorin who read through the manuscript and offered critical advice.

I thank the following for their words of encouragement: Hajia Nusirat Lawal, wife of the Executive Governor of Kwara State, Flt. Lt. M.U. Salisu (rtd), Alhaji Abubakar Jimoh and Mr Yinusa Yusuf.

Finally, I thank Almighty Allah for enabling me to realise my ambition of compiling these short stories. To Him is all glory. This collection is merely the drizzle that precedes the torrential rainfall. I hope, in the nearest future, to plough back its success with the hope of eventually reaping a bountiful creative harvest.

Isiaka Aliagan
Ilorin, January, 2000

Contents

Page

Acknowledgments		6
Introduction		9
1.	Time Rusts	13
2.	The Ripest Fruit	23
3.	Another Prey	29
4.	The Honeymoon	39
5.	Stifled Dream	55
6.	The Scars of the Moon	63
7.	A Gamble With Life	75
8.	Ordinance of Love	83
9.	The Hunter's Whistle	93
10.	Arrow of Fate	103

Introduction

For reasons not unconnected with the fast pace today of what Walter Ong calls "technologisation of the word," the short story genre is increasingly becoming popular with emergent writers in the nation. After his poetry collections, **Cadence** (1997) and **Emissary of Joy** (1999) Aliagan has responded to the vogue among his peers with this volume of ten short stories. While the debate continues on how long or short the short story is, the author's collection leaves no room for doubt, infused as his stories are with a pithiness and brevity that set apart species of the genre from long narratives.

The ten stories contained in this book avail readers with a kaleidoscopic picture of Nigerian experiences both in space and time. *Time Rusts*, the first story in the volume begins the author's exploration of linear as well as affective disjuncture between generations. The contemporary is seen interrogated about logicality, relevance and endurance in the depiction of the octogenarian Umu Sara and the rash juvenility of Bazage, her grandson. A similar concern with people, values and life of time past and present is seen to inform the author's motive in the experiences of characters in *The Ripest Fruit, A Gamble With Life* and *The Hunter's Whistle*. The emphasis however is more on the inherent values in rural life in the first and the last stories in the collection. Lara, the main character in the *Hunter's Whistle* is forced out of the university town, — simply called Central City — to Efomo in the rurality in search of solace from urban anxieties. In Lara's experience and that of the central unnamed person in *A Gamble With Life*, the author broaches the subject of the corrupt and debased life of urban dwellers in Nigeria.

Nigerians' notoriety for cheating and dubious deals in the nation's cities has since been recognised internationally. *Another Prey*, the third story in the book, presents what could qualify for an inside story of the infamous "419" (named after a legal clause enacted to curb the crime) a phenomenon which encompasses all forms of swindling and cheating.

In this story Adeyi, a retired public servant is swindled out of his only possession and source of livelihood by citizens, experienced and ingenious in acts of fraud and deception. The author's refusal to "drag" the Nigerian police into a crime of this magnitude speaks volume about the level of public confidence in the nation's law enforcement agents. *The Honeymoon* is another urban-international related story on a subject for which Nigeria is fast becoming notorious — drugs. A drug baron, Chief Adetoun, who loses a contest with the poet Makinde to marry Bola, is depicted with a vengeful scheme to get rid of the poet. The Chief's scheme is revealed overseas with Mrs. Davies and Austin at the centre of an international drug peddling when the newly-weds are enjoying their honeymoon. The dexterious, albeit obsequious ambassadorial diplomacy of Yusufu Ali-Biu gets the couple off the hook. With the happy rescue from tragedy of the couple, the author's art is also seen to be redeemed from a threatening pessimism.

Like the urban city, the university is often seen as the apex of the paradox of modern achievement and debasement. What motivates Lara in *The Hunter's Whistle* to voyage out from the city is seen again in Ansi and Hamida's recourse from the university campus to Dakata in *Ordinance Of Love*, namely the search for an unsullied atmosphere where man can be himself. The author thus reminds the youths that traditional values — always thought preserved in the uncivilised haven of the village — are not the same nor even compatible to modern democratic ideals which preach individual freedom.

The *Scars of the Moon*, the title story of the collection is, in style and imaginative depth, seconded only by *Arrow of Fate*, the last of the stories. While the former investigates the mysterious connection between the human mind and the moon, thereby drawing readers' attention to the etymology of "lunacy" and associated forms like "creative frenzy" and "possession by the Muse" which are associated with creative activities, the latter powerfully and emphatically preaches on the veracity of the religious or spiritual realm and, by that, the transience of human life.

By their focus on or reference to religious and unreal spheres of human experience, these two stories simultaneously reveal Aliagan's deeply religious orientation and his competence in handling, if he should wish, the Magical Realism genre.

For most critics, poetic thought and poetry constitute the manifestation of accomplished creative talents, followed in descending order by the short story, drama and the novel. But poetry is also known for its restricted, and in Nigeria today, diminishing audience. Consequently, contemporary Nigerian writers like Aliagan desirous of reaching out to a wider audience with their message are ever willing to halve their ante and minister to the Muse.

Saleh Abdu (Ph.D)
Department of English and European Languages,
Bayero University, Kano

Time Rusts

It was approaching noon. The atmosphere in Kanawo was serene but lonely. The streets were empty. The only sign of activity around the clan house was that of Abu Bazage and his pupils, Baba Sare and five youngmen at the weavers and Umu Sara, the purblind old woman seated in front of the clan house ruminating over the good old days and lamenting the rot that had become of life in Kanawo.

There were two main occupations in Kanawo, cloth weaving and pottery. In those days they were profitable trades. That was during the oil boom when most men thronged the cities in search of white-collar jobs. There was money then and most men returned to the community from time to time to purchase the *ofi* wears for various festivities.

The celebration was to last only for a while. The oil doom that followed shattered the trade, disintegrated most families and most young men grew disenchanted. They left the community in droves in search of survival as prices of *ofi* wears continued to nosedive.

Older men retired into dreaming and many sent their wards away in search of profitable trades. Many went away and never came back.

That was the beginning of communal decline in Kanawo. The past now could only be remembered with nostalgia. The worsening situation was beginning to sever family ties. In Abu Bazage's household, there used to be abundance of peace and contentment. When things turned worse, the family members became strangers to each other. One after the other, able bodied men began to leave.

The last of them, Bazage, was the hope of the old man. But what could Abu Bazage do when he had nothing to offer the perpetually restless youngman who had even been withdrawn from school because the fees could not be paid? It was only a matter of time for the lad too to succumb to the tide of the wanderlust.

Umu Sara had been brought out as usual to tan her wrinkled skin in the morning sun. Whenever the scorching effect of the sunray became too much, she was moved further into the shade provided by the roofing extension at the frontage of the house.

Umu Sara had been out about three hours already. This morning her mood was very critical. She was a fearless old woman who radiated a picture of awe. Umu Sara knew what everyone thought about her but she often remarked that she was the last of the link with the past; that she owed it a duty to the ancestors to ensure that the clan did not disintegrate.

She was very bitter about the turn of events. With just a little tribulation, her people had thrown in the towel and allowed the disintegration of the clan. She would continue to tell them the truth whether they liked it or not.

Umu Sara took her kola box from where she placed it. With an unsteady hand, she scooped some quantity of the mashed kolanut and thrust it into her mouth. Like she used to do whenever she was alone, she mused:

Umu Sara, that's my name. I am the oldest living being in this house. I have seen good and bad days. I have bore children and buried some. I have seen as many births as deaths in this house. I have seen joys and pains, and have tasted the varieties of all that life could offer. Nothing looks strange to me anymore.

Bazage is my grandson, a very likeable boy, not given to making trouble. You know this time was not like our time. Time changes people and people change time. I have seen some bad days. If it had not pleased Allah to take my sight I would not have been spared the agony of seeing the continued degeneration of our race.

I hear the voice of Dodo, the cloth weaver. Dodo, the crafty one. His father was my suitor. To think I could have mothered this man! Dodo, the funny character. He greets the blacksmith. He must have a tale to deliver, Dodo who relishes in probing people's privacy. May Allah shame the evil ones.

Thank God he is not coming my way. Who cries there? It's probably Muni's child. The brat. Why won't its mother go to her husband's place? In our time, no óne would do such a thing and not get banished. But time has changed. Kari would not even accept the paternity of the child. That's young people for you. They have desecrated the entire communal values.

They are as rotten as the time. Why do I even show such bitterness against these people? I probably am the one encroaching on their time. I should have no more business with the living. Why have I not died? That's the question on your lips. You like others consider me a witch; that I'm responsible for the misfortune of this house. Would it be my fault that I have lived to witness all these? Well, Allah knows the best.

I know I exist because of people like you. Bastard. The other time I fainted, all of you were jubilating that the old witch had gone at last. But it pleased Allah that my breath has not expired yet. You see your rotten life through what I say. You fear my sharp tongue that cuts through your decaying body like an incision. I'm simply your nemesis. Time that avenges all wrong done to life.

I swear by my grey hair that even Bazage could have been saved. I had warned his father, Abu Bazage, against sending him away. But he is my son; the only surviving fruit of my womb. Bazage is not only learned in the way of the whiteman, he had memorised the Koran at a tender age. We all predicted a buoyant future for him. He was going to be famous.

I had known he would go too. It is only a matter of time. Like all the others, he could not bear the acrid smell of the rotten time. How could he? Ha Bazage!

From the tone of his voice, Dodo is coming my way. The good for nothing infidel. He must be anxious to deliver his latest in town gossip. I shall not listen to him today. They must leave me to my thoughts. Now I feel an intense heat. Where is my fan? Who goes there? Yes, Kama bring me the fan. Where is your brother? Oh, you don't know. Okay, bring me water from the pot. I feel hot and thirsty.

Someone stoops before me. Ha, Dodo, so you've come? The devil. He will tempt me, I know. He prays Allah to spare my life but it is all hypocrisy. They wish I should die right now. They'll be happy for that. I ask him why he is not at work. He complains of backache. The crook. He goes about straightening his back by gossiping. He gives me kola. The crook bribes. Now I don't have an option. I must listen to him. It is his funeral, not mine.

Dodo speaks of the bad weather, the poor sales of ofi wears at the Iseyin market, about his little boy who had boil, his younger wife who quarelled, left for her parents' house and had refused to yield to intercession. By Allah, Dodo vowed to divorce his wife. Why is he bringing me into it? He wants my view so that when the marriage eventually collapses, they'll say Umu Sara, the witch caused it. Lord save me from them, you know Umu Sara is a good old woman.

Farther off, under the big guava tree, Abu Bazage sat with about two dozen pupils seated round him, learning the Koran. The tree provided shelter against the scorching effects of the sun. The shrill voice of the little ones pierced through the quietness of the noon. The pupils all held their brown slates marked with Arabic texts. Some of them held worn-out texts, torn in several places due to rough handling.

Abu Bazage held a long cane in his hand with which he enforced discipline among some of the urchins. Occasionally he would lash at a truant lad and in reaction the shrill voice of the reciters would rise in tempo, almost to a deafening pitch. This usually irritated him, and in annoyance, he would lash at several of the kids, shouting at them to keep their voices low.

It was about ten minutes to the end of the lesson. It was time to do a review of what had been learnt for the day. Abu Bazage beckoned at one of the pupils, Angulu. The boy, looking terrified, seized his slate and surged forward to meet the master. Abu Bazage never spoke but the boy understood the instruction. He began to read:

> *"Inna ansalinahu fi laitatul Quadri*
> *Wama adraika ma lailatul Quadri*
> *Lailatul Quadri akhaeru min alfishari... "*

Satisfied, Abu Bazage rubbed the lad's head. Angulu bowed and took his leave of the master. He called another boy, Ruba who also read his portion. After he had tested six boys, Abu Bazage concluded that it was time to let the pupils go. He called for the closing prayers and in chorus, the students chanted:

> *Praise be to Allah*
> *The Lord of all the worlds*
> *The beneficent, the Merciful;*
> *Owner of the day of Judgement,*
> *You alone we worship, you alone*
> *We ask for help.*
> *Guide us to the right path*
> *The path of those whom you have favoured*
> *Not the path of those who have*
> *Earned your anger, nor of those*
> *Who go astray.*

The pupils quickly deposited their slates in a large wooden box. The most senior of them collected the texts and took them inside the house. Like a burst dam, the urchins fluttered and ran in different directions away from the oppressive stare of Abu Bazage to the protective bosom of their mothers.

Abu Bazage stood up, stroked his beard and yawned momentarily. He had sat like that for the past six hours. He inherited the Islamiyyah school from his father of blessed memory at an age he was not quite ready for the task. Over the years however he had learnt the ropes. Pressing domestic demands had made things very difficult for him. Three of his four grown-up children had left in search of greener pastures. The last of them might soon go.

He strolled into the house and called his wife, Sali, to fill his kettle with water. The woman looked at him almost with disdain. Abu Bazage stiffened. He did not know what he had done to the woman. Despite his limited means he had always tried to satisfy her and her children. But to Sali he, Abu Bazage, was responsible for their misfortune.

Abu Bazage shook his head and headed for the back of the house to ease himself. By the time he came back, Sali had started crushing yam flour with pestle and mortar in readiness for their supper.

"Where is Bazage?" he asked.

"He should be at the field. You should know that, don't you?"

"Shut up. Don't you have manners? You are talking to your husband"

"Husband! What a husband?" she hissed.

Abu Bazage had to leave her. He did not want a scene. He went to his room. He was seething with anger. Why should that witch always challenge his authority? He was stupefied.

Abu Bazage only stayed indoors for a short while. After he had finished a bowl of *tuwo shinkafa* he had earlier sent one of the pupils to buy he decided to go to *Idi Ofi* to relax and wait for the afternoon prayers. Baba Sare and his four apprentices were there. One of them, Mufu, laid on his back and was snoring noisily, not bothered at all by the overpowering effect of the heat. Baba Sare was resting on his camp bed, with his smoke pipe dangling on his blackened lips. He had retired long ago from cloth weaving. Now he had boys in several places who worked for him.

The blacksmith was hammering away at the anvil. He fabricated all the weaving implements, from the wooden ones to the iron ones. His location near the weavers made things better. They could easily walk to his shed for whatever they needed. The clanging of iron against iron was almost deafening. Abu Bazage felt irritated, yet he did not want to go on any aimless stroll.

He sat there listening as the weavers gossiped about the troubled times and the aimless drift of the Kanawo people. Everyday someone vanished and most compounds were becoming deserted. Only the grown-up and the aged could be seen in most cases. There was a palpable air of gloom everywhere. Where would the old people go? They simply waited on time, and patiently for their death. Death was a common thing and sickness an everyday affair.

From mosque to mosque prayers were offered against delivery from the rot. There were more people in the mosque these days. Only the sick and the invalid abstained. After they said their prayers this afternoon, the Imam, a feeble old man took them on memory lane. In the past when something like that happened the pious and righteous clerics of Kanawo knew what to do. But now nothing worked; the present crop of clerics seemed to have lost the way.

Imam Sadiq spoke of the seventh ruler of Kanawo who had to sacrifice his life so that Allah might absolve his people from pains. It was during a time when the twin scourge of epidemics and famine ravaged the town and people were dying in multitudes like sacrificial beasts. He summoned the people to the praying-ground where publicly he asked the creator to take his life as ransom so that his people might live. It was not an expected thing and the people wept openly out of love for their respected ruler. He was a *waliyah,* the last of the greatest generation of the kings and shepherds. He died few weeks after the proclamation and the people survived the plague. In appreciation, the people broke the line of succession and made his oldest son the next ruler.

Night soon came and the people went to sleep with sorrow buried deeply in their hearts. Night brought temporary relief from daytime worries but the persistent heat made the comfort only short-lived. It was dawn and the muezzin's voice reverberated through the quietude, inviting the faithfuls to prayer. It was the first call, indicating that people could still catch some few more minutes of sleep.

Inside Abu Bazage's house, life had not fully returned. In one of the rooms where Bazage and some of his father's pupils slept, life was coming on gradually. In the room which stank of goat urine lay six young lads, including Bazage. The goat woke Bazage, having urinated on his trouser. Bazage was enraged as he felt the wet side of his trouser and cover cloth. But for his impending mission he would have gone after the goat.

Bazage stood at the door looking defiantly at the goat which appeared panting for want of breath from its race out of the room after Bazage gave it a rough kick. The lad changed his mind, went back inside to pick an unsoiled cover cloth. He went to the back-yard to clean himself and quickly performed his *dawn* prayers.

He had told Abu Bazage the night before about his plan to leave for the big city but the old man never responded to his statement. Abu Bazage never seemed interested in anything again. He had withdrawn totally into himself. He spoke only at the Koranic school when with his pupils. He never shunned company, only he rarely spoke. His mother, Umu Sara, had learnt to leave him alone too. That was his own way of reacting to the times.

Bazage dressed in his old school uniform and a grey trousers that had suffered from use. He never bothered to speak to his step mother, Sali. They were not on good terms anyway. So, it was not necessary. He avoided Umu Sara too because he did not want to see her disappointment. She would not agree he had to leave.

He took his only possession, an old Koran, an atlas book and a novel, *The Last Life*. The two books being prizes given to him at the end of the year examinations in Form Four before he was withdrawn from school when he could not pay the fees. The two prizes, he often held closely to his heart for they represented the relics of his aborted dream of going to school.

The young man took one last look at the smelling room, wondering when he would sleep in that room again. Somehow he felt no remorse in going away. He was going in search of life, in search of light. Kanawo held no promise at the moment. Things might improve in future. Allah knows the best. He passed through his father's door. It was still shrouded in solemn darkness with the light from the aged lantern almost dimmed into extinction. Bazage was surprised his father never woke up to observe his traditional pre-dawn prayers. Abu Bazage never missed the prayer and he woke up everyday at 3 a.m. for it. Was he afraid to witness his son's flight from the rot? Bazage shook his head, and went past the door into the gradually breaking day.

Abu Bazage did not come out for his Koranic lessons in the morning, he only directed the eldest boy to take charge. He was in a mourning mood. When the boys went to bring out Umu Sara for her sun-bathing, she was as cold as death. Cries, ululation, panic seized the air. Umu Sara had gone to join the ancestors. Within minutes Abu Bazage's house was besieged by a large crowd. Abu Bazage was forced to break his silence. He wept openly.

For the six days that the funeral lasted, no one knew the whereabout of Bazage. In the midnight of the sixth day, he surfaced. Bazage cried and blamed himself for the death of Umu Sara. He should not have gone away. For those who knew the bond between Umu Sara and the lad, they said she could not have lived, once her source of hope had been taken. Bazage vowed he would not leave Kanawo again. That was where his roots were and must remain.

The Ripest Fruit

A lone boy on a lone road trekked home one hot afternoon with sweat trickling down his small body in tiny rivulets. The boy walked on the empty street home, his small feet carrying him on with an apparent sign of fatigue and a disturbed mind. He walked in the hot afternoon sun, his school bag straddled at his back and a small wrapped parcel, his prize at the end of session examination, resting on his left arm. Toro trudged the brown-beaten path accompanied by a hollow silence.

Ahead of him was the long term holiday with its adventure and excitements. The school had just vacated for holiday. There was the usual end of session festival with cultural dances, drama presentation and award of prizes. Of course, there was the loving farewell speech of Lai, Toro's class mistress with whom the lad had grown intimate. But quite unusual the ceremony ended on a sad note.

That was the cause of Toro's sadness, the sorrow that marred the euphoria of his success at the examinations. Sometimes, he felt like shouting and jubilating that he had won, that he had made it but the thought of Lai depressed him. Poor Lai. Beautiful, simple and natural to the core. Her heart was filled with a fountain of human kindness. But intense sadness enveloped her entire life. Fate, of course, knows neither beauty nor kindness.

It was possible that Toro's mother, Maro, had something to do with Lai's affliction. He saw her having the fit for the first time that day. Since then it came on everytime. But today's own was the worst. In a gathering of teachers and pupils, it was the worst thing to happen to a beautiful person like Lai.

Toro's father was a blacksmith in the village. Most of the time he travelled to the surrounding villages to sell the farm implements fabricated by him. Whenever he returned from such journeys, Gogo usually came with a lot of articles for his family. From the moment he arrived to the time he embarked on another trip, there was usually festivity in his house.

This time Gogo came back with four bags of yam flour, two

gallons of red oil and a goat. He was angry when he did not see Maro turning up to help with the articles. Toro did not meet his mother at home so he had no word for his father who had been shouting her name. Toro struggled helplessly to pull one of the bags without success and the driver who was busy counting his money laughed at his frail effort. Musili, their neighbour's wife, later came to help the driver in taking the bags in. Toro happily pulled the yelling goat after him into the house.

His mother had gone to the tap since morning and noon was fast approaching and she had not come back. It was during the time water was as scarce as gold and fetchers had to queue, gazing at the water which flowed slowly like the blessing of God, waiting for their turn. There was an uproar as Toro approached the local tap. Two women were engaged in a duel. His mother and Lai of all people. As the two women fought with fingernails, Toro saw some of the people beating and tearing at Lai's dress from behind.

"This woman must be a witch. No wonder she is so stubborn and vicious," a woman whose face looked like that of a man said.

"People like her never marry," remarked Iya Rafa who sold beancake near their house.

"Beat her up," shouted a woman with a goitre extending from her neck. "Beat her, get the stick. The whip is medicine for madness," and she hit Lai on the head with a small wood.

Blood. The crowd quickly broke up. Lai's dress had been messed up. While a few sympathisers tried to clean Lai's forehead, someone quickly put her bucket at the tap. She had paid the price. No one disputed her right to take the water now. Toro looked at his mother's distorted face and he felt bitter. How could Maro descend so low!

To her mother's consternation, he volunteered to take Lai's bucket of water. He knew his mother never liked this but she did not say a word. She must have been regretting the fight now, Toro thought. Lai had just arrived the village and the school. She told the boy where she lived near the house of Tafa, the mat weaver. Toro knew Tafa very well. He usually passed by his shop whenever he went to the barber to have a haircut. There was a big bridge there that usually fascinated him as a child. That was where he was knocked down by a car when he was ten. He was lucky to escape with only a fractured hand. Since then he feared passing through that point.

They were about to cross the road now. The boy felt Lai's hand on his shoulder. He felt uneasy. The grip was harder now but he could not turn his head because of the weight of the bucket. Then he knocked his left foot against a stone and the impact sent Lai sprawled on the ground. Toro yelled and threw away the bucket of water. She was writhing and groaning on the floor and her eyes rolled menacingly as if they would come out. Her mouth foamed with a soap-like substance. Toro saw the bulge on Lai's forehead where the goitre woman had hit her.

"The mob. They have killed her!" Toro cried. "The crowd, they have murdered her!" he raved but the people who had gathered round them only looked ignorantly at him. They did not know what he meant. They would not know because they were not there. They would not know that the goitre woman had caused the damage which altered Lai's senses. The crowd was unmoved by Toro's outburst. They simply stared, not touching her. He wanted to touch her but a rough hand drew him back. Toro was perturbed. Why would they want Lai dead? What had she done to them?

The people at the tap were running toward them now. "The cannibals," Toro raved. "They'll kill her now," he cried and broke free from the man who held him to where Lai lay. He was stopped in time by Maro who had arrived the scene. She gave him a rough kick by the side and picked him up. Toro cried and struggled to disentangle himself from his mother's grip.

Toro saw them carrying Lai to a corner and covered her up. The horrific picture of death and corpse came to his mind. He wailed as his mother dragged him on, kicking whenever he tried to resist her. Toro refused to eat when he got home. When he came back, Maro told her husband of the tap incident and Toro's insistence on going with the afflicted woman. Toro was whipped for trying to bring a curse on the family and warned never to go near the woman again.

That night as he slept, wherever he turned he saw the beautiful figure of Lai in pain twisting on the floor. Her natty braids in shining strands now covered with sand and dust and her face contorted with terror. But when he saw Lai at school the following day it was as if nothing had happened to her. There was visibly no sign of yesterday's ordeal in her.

"I'm sorry for what my mother did to you," Toro apologised when he met her.

"Your mother is a nice woman. The fight only came because we misunderstood each other," she replied.

"And the mob ... " Toro began.

"We are all poor people struggling to live," cut in Lai. "And in struggling you don't always know when you are wrong or right," she explained. Toro was surprised at her answer. He had expected Lai to condemn them all.

"Are you really alright now?" he asked.

"Oh yes. You can see that for yourself. But don't let us talk too much about what is gone," she remarked.

That was how it happened the first time. Toro was convinced the goitre woman had altered Lai's senses with the wood. But today he had his doubt. What could be happening to Lai?

The sun was already moving westward by the time he arrived home. He met his mother settling a quarrel between the ever-fighting wives of Musa. Maro was the first wife in the family, hence she always arbitrated in all domestic disputes. At such time she was out of the reach of anybody until she had heard the last of the cases and passed a judgement. Toro sat by the pillar in the courtyard till Maro finished with the women.

When she was finally released, he ran ahead of her into the house, feeling relieved at last.

"I came first in the class again," he announced happily as soon as Maro came in. This same statement had been repeated for five years now yet it made no difference.

"Allah be praised," exclaimed Maro, raising her palms in prayers. Then she added: "The seer had said it all, your son will cross the sea to bring the knowledge at the other side of the ocean. He is destined to be great."

Toro watched his mother reeling out his praise names, praying for the fulfillment of the seer's prophecy. Toro's performance at school was one thing his mother loved him for. Aside from this, he was a rascal who gave her no rest.

Satisfied with her mother's appreciation, Toro now remembered Lai's predicament. "Mother, that teacher you fought with fell down again," he cut in.

Maro was silent, deep in thought. "But mother, can't we do something to help her?" Toro asked with the conviction that Maro should be able to help her.

"Helping a stranger who didn't ask for help can bring insult sometimes," remarked Maro.

"But..." began the lad.

"Listen, let me talk," countered Maro in a voice that was hardly hers. "Her sickness is the epileptic fit. No one knows of a permanent cure for it."

The realisation jolted the young boy. He had thought that the mob had wounded her in the brain. Toro left his mother, feeling demoralised. He felt her eyes following him as he left her room. Toro thought of Lai's predicament all day but found it difficult to reconcile with the cruelty of fate.

When she was in her best mood, Lai could pass for the best person in existence. She was the favourite of many pupils at school. Some who knew about the other side of her repulsed her good overtures. Toro had never seen Lai pining over this. Her face all the time wore charming smiles which suggested contentment with her fate.

Another Prey

It was a very chilly morning in Gbogunleri the third day since the harmattan started. The wind billowed through Adeyi's worn-out curtains, carrying with it powdery dust that had painted the floor, electronic appliances and furniture in the room in a white hue. It was the harmattan breeze that woke Adeyi. Somehow he did not take any precaution against the coming of the harmattan. His cover cloth appeared insufficient for the icy effects of the breeze. Adeyi yawned and stretched his hand to pick his wristwatch from under the pillow. The time was 8.25 a.m. Yet it was as though dawn had just broken. The middle-aged man could hear the sound of cooking made by his wife in the other room. Why had Maria not woken him up when he knew he had to go to work? He was about shouting her name when he remembered he had gone to bed with headache and a sign of fever. She might have decided not to disturb him. He struggled out of the bed and took his small radio by the window and started fiddling with the button. *"All flights to the northern part of the country were cancelled this morning due to the harmattan haze which reduced visibility to below 100 metres. Many passengers were stranded at the two terminals of the Murtala Muhammed Airport. Our correspondent who visited the airport said ... "*

That sounded like good news to Adeyi because it meant he had lost nothing that morning by missing the arriving passengers from both the north and the east. But it forebode bad news if no flight was recorded for the day. He placed the radio by the pillow, took his half-chewed stick and thrust it into his mouth. Downstairs, the Ghanaian shoemakers were having their early morning spree after a shot of the local gin, *ogogoro*. They must carry out the ritual before departing for the day's work. They danced to the Akwete sound, stamping their feet on the ground and dust flew about sticking on their overgreased body. Adeyi peeped through the parted window and saw the Hausa tailor and the chemist below him watching them with amusement. The Ghanaians were a happy, hedonistic lot; never given to brooding. They shake away their negative feelings by getting inebriated. To them if a day must start well, it should begin with dancing and drinking. He was still at the window when Maria came in with their last born, Tobi, apparently to wake him up.

"How was the night?" Maria asked him.

Adeyi spat out the saliva in his mouth through the window adjoining the pit.

"Fine, thank you. I feel alright now," he said.

He knew Maria would want to sweep the floor and dust the room. He took Tobi from her and went out to the balcony.

Instead of watching the Ghanaians, he went towards the pit, where all the faeces passed in the neighbourhood were deposited. He saw three swines scavenging on the waste. From the backyard he saw three men at the shower. One of them was singing and whistling as he bathed. Why had Adeyi exposed himself to this gory sight again this morning? He had vowed not to bathe in that house again, or go to shit in the exposed toilet, where the Ghanaians came to smoke *ganja*. Or where the lepers and destitutes came to bathe. It was the most dehumanizing thing to happen to anyone. Why had he descended to this bottomless pit? He who had lived with the civilised people. He now lived among the dregs of the society.

Adeyi was still lamenting his fate when the landlord came with a broom in his hand. "Excuse me teacher, I want to sweep where you stand," he said. To the landlord, Talia, every educated man was a teacher. Adeyi never bothered to correct him again. He had come to reconcile with the man's fate. Every morning he would sweep the balcony and the staircase because, as he said, he hated dirts. Everyone in the house believed Talia had been cursed with a bad spell during the contest for their late father's wealth, and that he would never improve.

Adeyi took Tobi back to the room and placed him on the bed. He called on Maria to bring his food. He took a jar of water and went to the balcony to rinse his mouth and wash his face. He came back to get dressed for work. After he had eaten, Adeyi took his car keys from where he hung it and went to say goodbye to his wife in the other room. He descended the staircase and greeted the wife of the chemist who met him at the door. The Ghanaians had dispersed. He stepped on the make-shift bridge constructed over the pit and started going towards Oniwaya and to come out at Capitol Road where he usually parked his car at night. The car must have gathered dust now, he thought as he approached the gate of the school. It was a good thing the school was on vacation, otherwise he would have caused a row for obstructing the movement of people.

"I think say you no go come today," the gateman told Adeyi as he stepped into the school's premises.

"No, mallam, I get fever small, na in causam," replied Adeyi and proceeded to tip the gateman with a five naira note.

"Haba, wallahi thank you. I am grateful. God go protect you. Nagode kware aboki na," greeted the elated Mallam Audu.

Adeyi cleaned the car. It was his only possession and he had protected it jealously since 1982 when he bought it. The car saved his life after he had been retrenched from the Federal Ministry of Works. Adeyi lost the grandeur of good living when he was asked to vacate their flat at the 1004 estate. Where could he have gotten ₦120,000 to rent a flat when he earned a paltry ₦3,250 per month? From a respected Senior Administrative Officer, Adeyi had degenerated to the scum of the society and had been forced to live among the poor at Gbogunleri where he could pay ₦200 per month for an indecent accommodation. Life had been difficult and he had to distribute his three other children among relatives. He had an aged bedridden father and a mother who lived on petty trading. When the going was good, Adeyi was the rallying point for all members of the family. There was a fraud in the Ministry and somehow unwittingly he was roped in. Even though he knew nothing about it the evidences of his collaboration were overwhelming. He had to go. He was a victim of his own carelessness.

Adeyi was on the road now. For about a week the car had been giving him problem. All his savings from the car hire business had been spent on reviving it. Adeyi could not afford to ground the car. It was their only source of living. As he drove through the Capitol into Agege Motor Road, Adeyi was thinking about what the day portended for him. He was praying that the weather situation would improve so that his family would have something to eat.

Traffic on the road was light. A few more minutes he would be crossing into the Airport road by the National Petrol Station after the bridge. As soon as he branched and had sighted the image of the dove, Adeyi was flagged down by a well dressed young lady.

"Okokomaiko, drop," she intoned.

"₦200," replied Adeyi who was happy that at least he would take something home. It was better than the ₦500 on the car hire service that might never come, he thought.

"₦150, I beg. You may even take me back if you wish," ventured the young lady.

"That makes it ₦300," added Adeyi.

"Okay, let's go," remarked the girl, and hopped into the passenger seat.

They drove straight and crossed towards the international terminal. In front of the arrival lounge, Adeyi saw the forlorn faces of his colleagues and silently he thanked God for his luck. There might be no flight today if the weather did not improve, he thought.

"You were late for work today. Most times you come before others," ventured the lady in a familiar tone.

The time was already 9.40 a.m. Adeyi looked at her.

"Do you know me?" he asked.

"Of course, you are one of the car hire people, and you are Mr. Adeyi," she replied.

He was surprised.

He turned to look at her but could not remember seeing her before." I don't remember meeting you before," he stated.

"You know Mama Jessica then. You and Mr. Martins used to come to eat at her place in Terminal One."

"O yes, I know her. Is that where you work?"

"No, I work at a salon inside the terminal and I do come there to eat too."

"Wonderful. The world is a small place. But I never noticed you before?"

"Well, I know you very well. You even took me and my Madam to Mile 2 once."

"Eh, so, why are you going to Okokomaiko? Are you not at work today?"

"I forgot the key to the salon. I'm going back to pick it."

"In that case I better hurry," he replied and accelerated.

They began to talk about the airport, the problem of the touts and the wranglings among the airlines, incidents of robbery at the airport and the pilfering of the navigational aids by hoodlums, luggage poaching and the recent shoot at sight order introduced by the government. The previous week, a night guard with the Airport Authority was murdered by robbers who came to steal runway light and cannibalised the only functional locator beacon. It was also a sad week for the aviation industry as it recorded one of the worst disasters at the Lagos airport. A BAC 1 – 11 aircraft belonging to Koloke Airlines caught fire after overshooting the runway. About 18 passengers died and many others were still in hospital receiving treatment for first degree burns and shock.

If Adeyi had the premonition of what was to happen he would have taken a clue from the problem the car gave them on the way. As soon as they passed NAHCO shed, the car began to jerk till it eventually stopped after the police checkpoint. He parked the car by the roadside, opened the bonnet and began to clean the fuel filter. It took him more than 45 minutes to work on the fuel pump and the carburetor before the car was revived. The rest of the journey was smooth except for the short delay at a traffic hold up caused by the roadmen at work at Toyota just below the flyover. They took a left turn by St. Leo's Church at Okokomaiko. The girl Roseline by now had made an impressive impact on Adeyi. She invited him into the house to take a bottle of coke before they commenced the return journey. It was a lightly furnished flat burrowed in the recess of the sparsely populated street. It was a new building, one of the several houses sprouting all over the outskirts of Lagos where Lagosians harassed by gluttonous landlords are beginning to find solace. Adeyi sat on the chair. Instead of a bottle of coke, Roseline came with two bottles of Big Stout and a glass cup. He was surprised how the girl came to know his preference. She only smiled, and replied that since she cared for him, she knew everything. Adeyi's mind began to imagine things. Roseline was not a bad girl afterall. It might do some good if they became intimate, he reasoned. He smiled. His mien indicated that their minds were working the same way.

Roseline came and sat by the arm-rest of the chair making sure that Adeyi took in an immeasurable dose of her costly scent and complementing that with some seductive touch. It did not take Adeyi a long time to sense the invitation. He began by placing his hand on her lap, then other things followed, till drunkenly they both retired to the bedroom to complete the act that spelt the doom. They lay on the bed exhausted after the overtasking rituals of love-making. Roseline's hand was resting on Adeyi's chest. This was the time most men fall to women's mischief. After a sumptuous carnal knowledge of a beautiful woman, most men would commit any fatal mistake no matter how wise they might be. Adeyi, by now, had convinced himself that if he had known Roseline earlier than now he would not have had any moment of sorrow. It would have been bliss all through. They just stayed there with Adeyi ready to forgo further work for the day. He did not want anything to take him away from the paradise lust. Just then they heard a key inserted in the lock at the front door. Adeyi stiffened and was rushing to get out of the bed. He was restrained by the girl. She told him the newcomer was her uncle she was staying with and that he would introduce Adeyi as her man-friend.

Uncle Tony as Roseline introduced him came into the house and saw a bottle of unfinished beer on the table. He sensed immediately that Roseline had brought a prey. "Roseline," he called from the parlour. Roseline who had dressed up responded that she was coming.

"Why are you not at work?" Tony asked.

"I came to pick the key to the salon. A friend brought me," replied the girl.

Adeyi could hear the conversation from the bedroom. He quickly got ready for the encounter. Roseline came into the bedroom to invite him to meet the uncle.

Just then, Rufus and a stranger came in.

'What happened?" Tony asked.

"Master, there is trouble," replied Rufus.

"We could not raise the ₦120,000 the customs people are demanding," he stated.

"How much have you collected?"

"Only ₦40,000. We need ₦80,000 more," he said.

Tony looked very disturbed. He held his head in his hands, appearing to be lost in thought.

"What do we do now? We may just lose everything. Goods worth ₦5 million."

They had some goods to clear at the port within 24 hours. Roseline was worried too. An intense silence pervaded the whole room.

"Uncle, why don't you go round to borrow the money," asked the girl.

"This is Lagos, Rose. How many people will borrow you money? Besides, it is risky because of the nature of the goods. You know it is contraband. The information should not get out of here."

He was silent for a while till something struck his mind." Rose, can you talk to your friend, afterall we are one now," Tony asked.

Adeyi was taken aback.

"Adeyi, please." Rose held his hand.

Adeyi surprised at having been brought in so suddenly took Roseline to a corner.

"You know I don't have that kind of money. Besides I was out of work for a whole week because the car was bad."

"You can borrow now. Don't forget all of us could become rich from this, and all this struggle will be over. Just raise something."

Adeyi remembered his eldest son's WAEC fees he had kept with someone, and the ₦7,500 he intended sending home to his mother in the village. All of that was just ₦12,500. May be he could borrow from his wife's money on her petty trading. He excused them and returned home.

The group quickly met when he left to perfect their strategy. Adeyi came back with ₦16,400. It obviously could not go far, Tony remarked. They had also raised ₦25,000. They added up everything and told Rufus and the stranger to leave immediately with the money. As soon as they left Roseline took Adeyi back into the bedroom where she gave him a treat that left him drained. Adeyi's head was spinning in the blues. He began to dream of a separated apartment to house Roseline as his mistress. Roseline herself told him it was good he met her uncle and that in a matter of days money would not be a problem again. Adeyi could retire from car hire business and start the real business of importation of jewelry, electronics, wears and apparels and so on. He begged Adeyi to do his best, saying that his contribution would determine his share in the booty. It took the people about two hours to return. They came back with a box. There were five boxes. The customs, they noted, agreed to release one box and insisted on getting the balance before the other four could be released. All the members of the group were aghast. It was a dead end. They resolved to sell the contents of the box to raise money for the balance. The box was opened but the contents were disappointing. It was filled with pieces of black papers which the stranger, who called himself Luke, called films.

"Who will buy this type of films and what is the value?" asked Tony.

"Master, first let's test its originality. Bring some *Omo* and water here," he directed.

Roseline ran to the kitchen and brought the two. Luke took a black bottle from his pocket and put a drop in the water mixed with *Omo*. Four pieces of films were thrown into the dish. All members of the group stood with apprehension, watching the transformation of the films. Instead of pornographic pictures what they saw were four ₦50 notes, new and fresh as any notes.

They exclaimed with disbelief. Money! Adeyi was alarmed.

Instead of the excitement which others exhibited he was seized by fear. He was afraid of the repercussion should the police get to know of what they were doing.

Tony quickly took control. "Gentlemen and lady, instead of pornography films what we have before us is money, bales of money. What do we do with this? Don't forget things have become more sensitive now; we need to handle this with care. Any slight mistake will be fatal. There is a tribunal in place for this kind of offence. The sentence for this is death; sabotage against the state," he sermonised.

Rufus came in. "At this stage, we all remain together. Any attempt to back out will spell doom. I suggest we discuss how to get this money processed and everybody goes away with his share."

"How many pieces in all?" asked Tony.

"500,000 pieces," replied Luke.

"Big money!" exclaimed Tony. "₦50 note in 500,000 places. That's big money enough to make all of us comfortable. Now, what's the way out Luke?"

"We need as much as ₦300,000 to procure the special chemicals to process the money," he said.

"Well, we sell whatever is sellable and get this money processed before tomorrow, "Tony concluded.

The target was Adeyi's car. They agreed to auction it with the electronics in the house. What was a rickety car to ₦5 million, thought Adeyi. By tomorrow morning, he would be a millionaire. He agreed to leave the car at Tony's apartment where the buyer would come for it. They agreed to meet in the morning at 6 a.m. to share the booty.

Adeyi left the group and started trekking towards the main road. Too many things preoccupied his mind now. What would he do with ₦5 million? He, Adeyi who had been confined to a life of penury, who lived with the dregs of the society, the scum of the earth at the dusty settlement of Gbogunleri. He saw his liberation in sight. Now his children would all go to school. He would escape finally from the scorn and sneer of his lunatic landlord, the jeers of his co-tenants who thought that with all his education he was no more than a driver. How life could treat an innocent soul! Adeyi took a danfo bus to Mile 2. From there he went to NAHCO shed where he joined the Airport shuttle bus to the local terminal. He went straight to the pepper soup joint. He had to think. He needed to raise up his mood so that his thinking would become clear. He ordered for a plate of the delicacy with a bottle of big Stout. That would be his third bottle for the day. Adeyi was merry.

"Final announcement on flight OY 092 to Yola and Maiduguri," the announcer's feminine voice came through the air. Adeyi looked around, as would any concerned passenger. "Due to the inclement weather condition, this flight has been cancelled. The management of Koloke Airlines regrets the disappointment caused our passengers. If you have purchased ticket on this flight, kindly proceed to our ticketing counter for your refund. Thank you."

There was a murmur of disappointment from the stranded passengers. At the risk of their lives some of them would be ready to go on board and dare the elements. The environment became noisy. After Koloke's announcement came that of Zenith and Triax. One after the other all the airlines announced the cancellation of their flights. Adeyi was glad he was not at work. As he sat there savouring his plate of pepper soup and watching the *Black Ninja* film on the video at the joint, he never knew he had just mortgaged his future.

As soon as he left the group, Tony, Roseline, Luke and Rufus all jumped into his car and headed toward Badagry en route Cotonou where they would get a good buyer for the salon car. The house they used for the operation had been unoccupied for two years and the furniture were rented for the operation. Roseline only spied on him. She never worked in the airport. She had been on his trail for the past two weeks. The gang of four after an accomplished deal went after another prey. In a day, Adeyi lost what he had protected and guarded jealously for 15 years. He lost not just his job but his senses. He lost control, the following morning at 6.00 a.m. when he arrived the house to collect his share of the booty and met an empty space, everything gone. Instead of asking for his car, he ran helter-skelter, saying he had been robbed of ₦5 million. His driver-colleagues at the airport took him, contributed some money and advised his wife to take him home to a native doctor before he became permanently insane. Only Adeyi knew the story of the ₦5 million and could only tell it if ever he regained his senses.

The Honeymoon

The aircraft had just taken off from the Rio de Janeiro International Airport. It was a Varig Boeing 747 operating flight 042 to Lagos. The flight was a full house, comprising mainly of tourists and the regular business class who came to Brazil at frequent intervals. The jumbo jet had gained a comfortable altitude, its nose-cone, like a proboscis, probing the vast skyline and skirting the bank of the Copacabana Beach, one of Brazil's 2,000 beaches, spanning three kilometers..

There were over 400 passengers in the roomy cabin. A few of them were engrossed in scanning the landscape, the mountains and the beautiful scenery below. They scarcely paid attention to the flight instructions relayed through the cabin video, extending from the wall partition segmenting the cabin into three classes. Makinde and his wife were ensconced in their cushioned seat in the club class. The new bride exhausted by the shopping spree they undertook shortly before departure was snoring coolly like a new airconditioner wary of drawing attention. The couple had spent one month in the city on their honeymoon and were returning home to resume work.

The power of the cooling system in the cabin had increased in intensity. Pressurised air now billowed like cauldron smoke, filling the cabin with chilled vapour. At this point, the passengers began to settle down for the eight-hour flight across the Atlantic Ocean. A cabin attendant announced through the overhead communication gadget that inflight games and relaxation materials would soon be distributed. She wished the passengers a smooth and enjoyable flight.

Makinde cast a brief glance at his wife and smiled with grateful satisfaction. Bola looked innocent and babyish as she cuddled herself into a protective cocoon, enjoying her well-deserved nap. He picked up an inflight journal and began to read it. It was the article on *Rio, an Apotheosis of Nature* that interested him. Makinde loved wildlife preservation and nature conservation. He believed the world was drifting too much into artificiality through the destruction of man's natural culture, habitat and history. He read on...

Soon they would be out of the Rio airspace. Makinde's mind began to weave a poetic verse. He turned to the aircraft window, looking down at the vast landscape with human beings treading on them diminishing into tiny reptiles. His lips began to twist, his vision taut and he fixed his eyes on the wing of the aircraft as it cut through the layers of the clouds. The weird poem he had created began to take shape. With a pencil he began to scribble the poem on the edge of the inflight magazine:

> *In the void*
> *there is nothing*
> *but pale white*
> *and blue nothingness*
>
> *Up among the void*
> *it is numb*
> *in the flying cabin*
>
> *So it is numb and*
> *void like*
> *life made of*
> *pure red earth*
>
> *The red clay too*
> *suspended below*
> *is void*
>
> *The hairy earth*
> *looks bald like*
> *A barren terrain*
> *that is void of produce*
>
> *Through a mountain*
> *of voidlike*
> *cotton wool, we're*
> *flying...*
>
> *Ascending, descending*
> *inside the hollow tummy*
> *of the flying elephant*
> *that looks like a coffin*
> *in which a void is kept.*

He read the poem over and over again. He was not yet satisfied. He would definitely return to it, he told himself. Now his mind began to stray and his eyes strained. Makinde looked at the sleeping Bola and he felt he owed her everything for the complete wholeness he felt now. He had been shaken to the roots when a few weeks to the tying of their nuptial knot, some members of her family had tried to ditch him in favour of one Chief Adetoun who had lavished them with money. Makinde almost lost his love. Only six months out of Lagos on course in Boston had almost ruined his chance. The young man had worked desperately hard to reclaim his love and had vowed to make Bola the happiest woman on earth to shame those who had tried to separate them. To him Bola was a jewel, and he had been favoured by love and luck to win her.

Bola had remained loyal and devoted to him throughout the travails. Then Makinde thought, "she is aware of my inadequacies in certain aspects, yet she is ready to live her life through with me." He felt her understanding and unflinching solidarity with him must be borne out of the philosophical conviction that there was no imperfection in what was appreciated. Bola looked completely serene and out of tune with any worldly worry. "How different we are," Makinde thought again, "but brought together by a common faith in love, believing that love is a miracle capable of fusing two diametrically opposite people together into a complete being. Love certainly knows neither creed nor clans, neither tribe nor topography. Love is sublime, love is supreme."

"Tea or coffee?" the beautiful air hostess who had come to serve them asked on getting to their seat. Makinde was brought back to the cabin world.

"Coffee," he replied and smiled at the ebony black Brazilian girl. He would prefer coffee instead of tea. He wanted to be alert throughout the flight. The strong Brazilian coffee would clear the drowsiness he was beginning to feel. The airconditioner's cold effect was becoming unbearable for most passengers. Hot towels were being passed around for passengers to mop their faces and massage their numbed fingers.

"Obrigado," Makinde thanked the hostess in one of the few Brazilian words he had been able to pick during their one month stay in Rio.

"Obrigado," intoned the hostess with a broad, disarming smile, and pointed at the sleeping Bola, asking whether she needed anything. Makinde told her she was alright. The hostess asked him if he needed anything more to which he nodded no. But she soon returned with a blanket for the sleeping Bola to minimise the cold from the airconditioner. Makinde was more than grateful. How altruistic Brazilian girls could be, he thought.

He was still looking at the receding back of the hostess when he remembered his encounter with another Brazilian girl at the Sugar Loaf Mountain where he bought a tee-shirt for Seun, his little in-law and favourite.

"Ten dollars for a tee-shirt?" Makinde had asked the fair bikini-wearing youngster selling the clothing.

"This beautiful. Ten dollars, small price okay," the girl ventured in a smattering English, to the amusement of Makinde who was holding the tee-shirt, admiring it and not wanting to relinquish it.

"I will pay five dollars and nothing more," he insisted, although he knew the price should be more than that but that was what he had on him. Bola who had the rest of the money with her had a phobia for height and tall structures and had opted to stay back.

"You crazy? This for five dollars? No, no, no," the youngster exclaimed, snatching the clothing from him. Makinde was annoyed and would have left in that state. He could not read the humour in the youngster's insistence.

"Look, me crazy to sell this five dollars. Amigo take this eight dollars. I sell this to go to school, okay," she offered now in a pacifying tone.

Makinde had still not collected the tee-shirt. "So you go to school?" He asked as a matter of interest.

"Yes most Brazilian womans here and girls go to school," she pointed at the other girls.

"So?" Makinde laughed. His ribs ached and tears came out of his eyes. The youngster laughed too. Then she thought something about her must be amusing. Her manner of speaking perhaps. "Now Amigo pay eight dollars, customers plenty," she offered.

"Okay friend, I have five dollars here. Honestly, I would have paid more," Makinde said between his laughter. His eyes glistened with spots of tears. He cleaned his eyes with the sleeve of his shirt.

"Alright, bring that. You crazy I know," the youngster said with a smile, tapping the front pocket of Makinde.

"Which school do you attend?" Makinde asked after collecting the tee-shirt and paying her.

The girl, Paula, did not reply him. Instead she asked, "You Nigeria?"

"Yes," Makinde replied her with excitement, surprised at the girl's ability in guessing his nationality right. There were only a few blacks at the Sugar Loaf that morning.

"You Nigeria, ah, ah," Paula laughed. Then she was serious, her face crossed with an unfinished laughter. "You Nigeria, I know. You got petrol," she started counting her fingers as if enumerating the number of barrels produced per day. "But you crazy," she quipped.

"You crazy," Makinde found himself telling her. They both laughed.

"But you crazy I know," she insisted.

"You crazy, too to wear that," Makinde pointed at her bikini which made her half-nude.

"You crazy," the youngster mimicked and she was gone. Makinde saw her running after another customer. He turned away amused by what the youngster had said. "Does she know what it means to be crazy?" he asked himself. "The girl should be joking," he assured himself. She probably picked the slang from somewhere and it became a part of her.

He was still thinking about the endless crypt called life when the cabin attendant called for their attention and he asked in his mind, "must they announce everything they have to do?"

"Ladies and gentlemen, Captain Milo requests for your attention please," she repeated through the overhead speaker. There was a surge of murmur in the cabin. "Captain Milo requests your attention, ladies and gentlemen, there is an important announcement," the cabin attendant said once again. This time, most passengers, including those who had been sleeping became alert. The four whitemen who had been drinking since take-off from Rio also became serious for once.

"Hey men, what sort of Captain is this? He is supposed to be quiet throughout the flight. This is the second time he would be speaking," one of the whitemen said in a voice gone husky due to excessive drinking.

"Joe, what do you think is happening?" the other one asked in response to the question.

"I think the guy is simply tired like us and wants a chance to pull up and rest," replied the humorous member of the group and the whole cabin roared with laughter.

The cool confident voice of the Captain came through the overhead speaker. "Ladies and gentlemen, my name is Captain Etienne Milo. I'm in command on this flight. It has been a normal flight and everything is going on well. But we have to return to Rio for security reasons. The Federale Policia has requested that this aircraft return to base due to certain emergency. Please bear with us. We'll resume the flight as soon as we're cleared," he concluded and clicked, the microphone went off.

Silence descended on the cabin. The atmosphere was so still that a drop of pin could have drawn attention. It was already about 25 minutes airborne, and there had been no apparent sign that the flight would be aborted. Several thoughts dominated the minds of the passengers. Could it be a case of hijacking? But as no hijacker showed up, the thought was discarded. Could it be engine failure? someone asked. No, the plane was maintaining a stable course. The aircraft glided on air like a giant whale as if unperturbed by the worry of the passengers. No one knew why the aircraft was called back to base. No one, including Makinde, knew that sitting behind them were two drug couriers, and that the Brazilian Police were acting on a tip-off.

The 25 minutes turn around time filled the passengers with apprehension. The cabin crew had abandoned the aircraft aisle. No one wanted to answer questions on why the plane was being turned back. The return flight progressed steadily without any communication between the cockpit and the cabin. The Boeing 747 began a gradual descent now. This time, the city lit up at night did not paint a carnival look. The lights were subdued and gloomy like the flickering rays of funeral candles. No one expected any cheering news on landing. The runway lights had shown now, serrated on the asphalt darkling like race tracks. The pilot skillfully brought the aircraft down and then began the landing roll, taxying to the tarmac before bringing the plane to an ominous halt at the apron.

There were some other wide-body jets on ground with the familiar livery of the British Airways, Lufthansa, KLM and some other Brazilian domestic airlines, including TAM. As soon as they alighted from the aircraft into the D Finger, the anti-narcotics squad and security operatives stormed the aircraft. They combed through the cabin with sniffer dogs on the trail. The returning passengers, oblivious of the culprits among them submitted themselves for screening. Bola clutched at her husband's arm on the queue as hand luggage were checked and the anti-narcotics squad leafed through the checked-in baggage at the apron.

It was all done within 15 minutes, and the culprits were already picked out like jiggers from an afflicted foot. Makinde and Bola had been cleared, and were waiting, like others, for the resumption of the flight. They never knew their connection with the search until a security personnel came for Makinde. The young man was too surprised and alarmed. He was livid with rage but the security man held on. Bola was awestricken. She began to wail, calling for help. The entire departure hall was thrown into an affective emotional outburst. Makinde looked around, stupefied by the scene. He could not understand anything. More personnel of the Federale Policia came out now. Then the young man sensed the impotence of his fury.

"Calm down darling, don't you worry," he placated his wife. "I will soon be back. They should know we have no connection with all this," he explained, easing out Bola's grip on his arm and urging the officer who held him to move on.

It was when Makinde got to the office of the Brazilian Police that the whole thing dawned on him. There in chains were Mrs Kokuma Davies he had helped to clear her excess luggage and the lad, Austin who had chatted with him before the check-in. It was then the jingle DO NOT TAKE LUGGAGE FROM A STRANGER. YOU MIGHT BE TRICKED INTO BECOMING A COURIER OF HARD DRUG made sense to him. He looked at the two, and hot blood of vengeance rushed through his vein. He screamed invectives at them, cursing them in his native dialect. The police merely looked on at the ensuing drama. Makinde was handcuffed. All appeals that he should be allowed to discuss with his wife was turned down. He no longer believed he would be let off the hook. There and then, his fate appeared to have been sealed.

Flight 042 was eventually cleared for take-off after about two hours on ground. The passengers were infuriated by the delay. Only a few still remembered the young couple on honeymoon implicated in the drug trafficking. The flight took off 10 o'clock Brazilian time but this time without the couple on honeymoon and the two drug couriers. Bola had declined following the flight. How could she with her husband in the dungeon? Several gloomy thoughts played in her mind. How would she cope with the sneer of those who were opposed to her marriage to Makinde? What about the leering snide of Chief Adetoun? Bola felt dejected and disoriented. She sat glued to a spot, her chin resting on her palm, lost in thought. Airline officials had to phone the Nigerian Embassy in Sao Paulo to come and pick their distraught citizen.

Ambassador Yusufu Ali-Biu himself took the call. The other

embassy staff had all gone. Now Ambassador Ali-Biu stayed late at the office. With the rumour of impending redeployment of some ambassadors on air, he was not willing to risk any chance. He felt he must convince the authorities in Lagos that only a strong person like him could hold forte in a country like Brazil. Moreso, with the drug trade reaching an alarming proportion, and Nigeria gradually turning into a market for the narcotics instead of a transit point, the government in Lagos had given each ambassador abroad a special task to uncover Nigerians involved in the drug racket, or lose their jobs. Now this particular case interested Ambassador Ali-Biu. Couple on honeymoon caught with heroine, he reasoned, would be a good weekend menu for the government and a fascinating headline for the junk magazines circulating all over Lagos. Ambassador Ali-Biu decided that he would fly to Rio that night. Before leaving he sent a telex to Lagos: SEVENTH CASE IN ONE WEEK, COUPLE ON HONEYMOON CAUGHT WITH HEROINE. HUSBAND ALREADY DETAINED. PLEASE STEP UP CAMPAIGN AGAINST DRUG TRADE, he seemed to plead, but Ambassador Ali-Biu was enjoying the show. It would teach the *babariga* boys in Lagos that it was not easy being an ambassador, being a Nigerian ambassador, he meant.

Ambassador Ali-Biu had served in six countries: Cuba, Lebanon, Central African Republic, India, Kuwait and Iraq. He came to Brazil from Iraq shortly after the cessation of the Iran-Iraq war. Ambassador Ali-Biu liked serving in hot spots. With threats of sanction from western nations due to the continued arrest of Nigerians with the dangerous drugs and the latest concentration of Nigerian couriers in Brazil, the Ambassador had taken the war against drug trade as his chief occupation. The government in Lagos had stepped up campaigns nation-wide, and used international media to fight against the threatened isolation of the country by the international community.

In recent times pilots, flight engineers, cabin attendants, military personnel, politicians, sportsmen and religious leaders had been arrested at the nation's premier international airport in Lagos. Foreign citizens had been docked and convicted for drug crimes. A few aircraft had also been impounded by the nation's aviation authorities in connection with carriage of drug couriers. Ambassador Ali-Biu knew that any ambassador not sensitive to government's feelings about the drug trade was playing with his job. He flew to Rio that night to take the distraught girl into custody and begin investigation into her husband's case.

That night inside the dingy police cell, Makinde's mind was in turmoil. His inability to communicate in Portuguese made matters worse for him. He was worried about the state of things and what was happening to his wife, Bola. The cell was dark. The only reflection of light came from the corridor. It was a small room but the ventilation was not bad. Makinde was weighed down by the yoke of desertion. He had requested for a biro and paper to put down his statement but with the poor light, he would not be able to write anything. Makinde blamed himself for yielding to the advice of his wife to help the woman who had put him in trouble. Mrs Kokuma Davies: who could have thought she was a courier of hard drug? How low some human beings could descend! And the boy, Austin, who said he was doing his Masters at the Sao Paulo University. Such a boy, he thought. What sort of dreams do young men have these days? Makinde sat on his bed, his heavy eyes focused on the doorway as if a Messiah would come in from there. His mind then strayed to a few hours before their departure at the airport terminal.

The departure hall that evening was a beehive of activities. Intending passengers filled the hall to the brim and luggage occupied nearly all the available space. There was an atmosphere of celebration and most people radiated an air of satisfaction from an accomplished business deal, or from simple sensual satisfaction. There were many familiar faces, most of them co-passengers who came on board the same flight a month earlier. Some of them were familiar faces he met at the beach, the Corcovado Mountain ---- site of the Christo Redento Statue, the Sugar Loaf, Maraçana Stadium, the Botanical Garden or Rio Sul ---- the magnificent supermarket. Most of the intending passengers were sharing their one month experience at the Carioca city. That was when Mrs Davies approached Makinde and Bola. Both were discussing in their mother tongue when the lady dressed in Yoruba *adire* attire came to them.

"Good evening uncle," she greeted Makinde, then turning to Bola, she ventured, "Madam, how are you?"

"We are fine, thank you," Makinde answered, returning her greetings. "Pleased to meet you. Makinde is my name and this is my wife, Bola," he added, glad to have met someone from their native environment.

"I'm Mrs Kokuma Davies," replied the middle-aged woman. "I

come to Brazil every month, is this your first visit?" She asked the couple.

"Yes, we are on a honeymoon." It was Bola who answered her, feeling proud with that revelation.

"Oh sorry, I didn't realise that," Mrs Davies interjected. "Accept my congratulations on your wedding. I wish you a happy marital life," she prayed, offering her handshake for the second time, and both parties were quite happy.

"Thank you madam. We are indeed happy to meet you. Thanks for your company," Makinde enthused. They were soon on a very intimate level. They chatted on from one topic to another. The fact that they came from the same state excited all of them. The world was such a small place, they seemed to reason. Mrs Davies said she was a widow and had taken to business to sustain her three children, two boys and a girl at the university in Ibadan.

It was getting to 5.00 p.m. In another 30 minutes, the check-in formalities would commence. The couple were quite at home with their partner. It was the first time since their arrival in Brazil that they would communicate with any one in their native dialect. Midway into their discussion the lad Austin came to introduce himself. He was a young boy of about 24. He claimed he had met Makinde somewhere but he could not be sure of the exact place. Makinde agreed they could have met, after all the world had been reduced to a global village. He liked the boy and he did not mind his company

Austin soon suggested that they had a stroll round the terminal. They took a short detour and ended up at a cool spot. Makinde was glad at the interlude and a short break from his wife who was a strict disciplinarian. Since meeting her, Makinde rarely touched the bottle. His old interest got a boost when Austin mooted the idea that they had a drink. He took a glass, careful not to get inebriated. While on the drinks, they chatted on from economics to politics. The nation, they both agreed, was on the precipice of collapse. The military government that just handed over power had pillaged the treasury, and left empty coffers for the politicians who immediately on assumption of office went on a borrowing spree. They painted red all the finance houses in London and Washington. The national debt, it was said, was so huge that three hard working generations would not be able to clear it. Unemployment, crime, and other social ills were at an alarming peak. Youngmen took to drug trafficking to amass wealth. There were rumours of another coup to disband the politicians but these were mainly rumours speculated every now and then by the media. Only God knew what was going on at the Dodan Barracks. And unless there was a martial song, or there was a coup tribunal, all news on coup remained speculations.

"It is a vicious circle," remarked Makinde. "The problem remains no matter who stays up there."

"Maybe our Messiah too will come one day. Other nations have had it worse but they endured and overcame their problems," the boy Austin contributed.

"Well there is value in hope, no one can quantify that," Makinde agreed. "But hope where there is no light at the end of the tunnel is delusion, and it could have a calamitous consequence which can shake the fabrics of our existence," he stated.

"Still there is nothing like hope," Austin insisted. "It costs nothing, so if it produces nothing, then nothing is lost." They both laughed at the strangeness of the boy's statement.

It was not long before the check-in announcement was made for the Lagos-bound passengers. The two men rose and made their way to the counters. It did not occur to Makinde that both he and his wife had been playing their part as cast in a calamitous drama. When they got to the counters, Austin left them under the pretext of going to change his dollars to Cruzeiro so that he could pay for the airport tax. Mrs Davies too having worked on Bola said she was going to the ladies.

"You took beer," Bola challenged her husband in reproach as soon as he sat down. His breath apparently stank from the alcohol he took.

"Sorry dear, it was a mistake. That boy lured me and somehow I couldn't resist," he pleaded feeling stupid. Taking her hand, he whispered placatingly "you know I didn't drink since we came here." "Yes, you didn't. This one, the boy lured you, a mere boy isn't it? Anyway one day someone will lure you into something regretful if you don't learn to resist," she admonished but there was no bitterness or anger in her voice. After all, Makinde was the man and she the woman. But Makinde was silent. Sometimes he felt weak whenever Bola reproached him for a wrong doing. Sometimes she acted as if she were his mother, always putting him right. Perhaps that was what women were created for, he thought. To put men aright when they went astray. Sometimes they led men astray when they were on the right lane, Makinde's other mind told him.

"Anyway let's forget that. That woman, Mrs Davies needs our assistance. I promised her I'll talk to you about it," Bola said, changing the pattern of the talk.

"Ah I no get money again o!" Makinde exclaimed in the Nigeria's corrupted version of the Queen's English.

"Yes I know. It has nothing to do with money," Bola explained. "She simply wants us to help her with an excess luggage to avoid paying more. You know we don't have much."

"Hmm," Makinde sighed. He did not like the idea. "Dear, we have just met this lady, why do you think we should go to that extent helping someone we hardly know?" he asked.

"No darling, it's not like that. Remember we had a similar problem when we travelled to Paris. At the Charles de Gaule, somebody bailed us out when we had a similar problem. Don't be ungrateful to God. It is our turn to help somebody," she preached.

Maybe she would be offended if he did not agree. Makinde too did not sense any danger, after all the lady had been kind and sociable. As if watching them from a distance, Mrs Davies suddenly appeared. Makinde checked in her bag in his name and the luggage tag was fixed on his ticket. That was how he was tricked into being a courier of hard drug.

Makinde thought over the event and he felt both foolish and bitter. He would deal with Mrs Davies and Austin if he had the chance. Why did they not exonerate him? What had he done to deserve this kind of treatment? Makinde felt betrayed. How could he have known that the lady and Austin knew each other? God would surely intervene, he suddenly went sober, succumbing to the religious belief that God would never leave the innocent to suffer. Makinde's vision was clouded. From his mind's eye, he pictured his wife cracked down by the sad realisation that he had fallen into a trap set for both of them. Bola would grieve more because she was the primary instrument of Mrs. Davies' deceit. Perhaps if she did not insist, it would not have come to this.

The young man stood, walked unsteadily towards the lone table and chair in the cell. He stooped, then knelt and placed his two hands wet with his own bitter sweat upon the chair and prayed. Makinde prayed like he never prayed before but God did not seem to answer his prayer. God probably had a reason. But God's way was not the way of man. God's way was incomprehensible and unpredictable. Mrs Davies and Austin refused to exonerate him, and the police would not believe he knew nothing about the drugs.

Only God could intervene but he had not heard from God. Makinde waited in the dingy police cell.

Three days passed and Makinde was still detained in the police cell. His wife was allowed to see him only once. Ambassador Ali-Biu had thrown his diplomatic weight behind the case and hired the most brilliant lawyer around to defend Makinde. But he who must go to equity must go with a clean hand. Makinde's hand had been soiled. Only the confession of the two drug couriers could prevent him from being sent to the gaol. Three days in incarceration had humbled the young banker. He was no longer irascible. He bore his fate stoically like a true devotee of pains. Someday, he still thought, they would let him off the hook. The presence of Ambassador Ali-Biu made the matter easier for him, and the Federal Policia were careful lest they sparked off a diplomatic row which would not be easily doused.

Bola fought her husband's battle gallantly like a devout wife. She moved from one association to the other, human right groups, the Black Fraternity, and Nigeria United, and campaigns were carried out in the media and several rallies held in front of the Nigerian Embassy in Sao Paulo. The Ipiranga Avenida, venue of the court proceedings, was besieged with placard carrying youths, all proclaiming the innocence of the young Nigerian banker. It was not the protest alone that did the magic but the eventual confession of the two drug couriers after serious torture. Mrs Davies confessed that she and Austin were hired by Chief Adetoun, Makinde's rival, to plant the drug in Makinde's luggage or to use him to clear the heroine. They explained that Chief Adetoun had a score to settle with Makinde for humiliating him out of the contest for Bola's love.

Makinde was freed on the seventh day of his arrest. There was a celebration at the Nigerian Embassy, and the Ambassador seized the opportunity to address the media. Yes the authorities in Lagos would know he was not an armchair ambassador. Ambassador Ali-Biu was a man of action. He warned Nigerians resident in Sao Paulo and elsewhere in Brazil to beware of friends. He noted that in the drug pushing business the most unsuspecting people had landed innocent persons in trouble. He told them that desperate drug couriers had stuffed the tummy of dead infants with narcotics substance, some swallowed the substance while others stored it in detergent packs. He warned them against leaving their luggage unguarded. That day, Ambassador Ali-Biu sent another telex message to Lagos. NARCOTICS SQUAD SHOULD HUNT FOR

DRUG BARON, CHIEF ADETOUN, CHAIRMAN TOUN MOTORS. MAKINDE WAS ONLY A VICTIM OF REVENGE.

It was a harrowing experience for the couple. Their honeymoon had been shattered with the unfortunate event. But they still thanked God who had sent a Messiah, through Ambassador Ali-Biu, to bail them out. Makinde's faith in God was rekindled. At a moment he had resigned himself to fate, believing that only a miracle could bring him out of the ordeal and the trap set by the vicious Chief Adetoun. The couple spent two more days in Sao Paulo, recuperating before they began preparations for the long journey home.

This time it was a DC-10-30. Varig alternated between the Boeing 747 and the DC-10 jet. There were only 240 souls in the cabin. The cabin was narrower and not as roomy as the jumbo jet. The Captain was reading the flight instruction through the cabin video. The plane would be cruising at 35,000 feet above the sea level in an eight hour flight across the Atlantic Ocean. The instruction did not make much meaning to the bruised couple sitting on seat number 14a and 14b. Their horrible ordeal with the drug couriers had left a sour smell in their mouth.

Their big Oriental bag had been seized as exhibit. They had only their hand luggage which contained a few essential items. Ambassador Ali-Biu was talking of pressing for compensation on unlawful detention but Makinde was more interested in his freedom, and he had got it. His mind was now on Chief Adetoun and he promised to even the matter with him. Makinde did not know the man could be so mean. Maybe all rich men were mean and vicious, he thought. Anyway he thanked God that the whole scheme failed. Where would he have been now? Had the ambassador not intervened, what would have happened? He, Makinde, would have been sent to jail for an offence he did not commit. He sighed and shook his head. All the while his wife was looking at him. Bola had still not been able to say anything about the traumatic event.

Makinde pulled her to him. He could see she was about to break in tears. He cleaned her soft face with an handkerchief and kissed her lightly on the lips. "It's alright. Everything is now alright," he said patting her on the shoulder. "This is the second test on our love," he said, "but on both occasions we triumphed. We'll definitely live longer than our enemies. True love waxes stronger in moments of adversities. I know we'll never be separated. The enemies are only trying their best."

"You're an angel Makinde. I can never leave you," said Bola, her voice heavy with suppressed tears.

"I do love you Bola. We shall remain together forever, come what may," he said solemnly clasping her soft, warm hand in his. He could feel warm currents travelling through his veins. The couple were not interested in the world of the cabin people. They were interested only in their own world of renewed love and faith in each other. Nights of insomnia soon began to tell on their fatigued body. They soon drifted into a smooth fitful sleep, their suffering and worry flowing out through the air they exhaled from their noses. They breathed in fresh air of freedom. At the background, Madonna's *La Isla Bonita* was reaching them like music from the blues.

I prayed that the day would last
they went so fast,

Tropical highland breeze,
all of nature wide and free
This is where I long to be
La Isla Bonita.

And when the samba played

The sun would set so high and ring my ears,
and sting my eyes,
your Spanish lullaby.

I fell in love with San Pedro
Warm wind carried on the sea...

Stifled Dream

It was 10 p.m. and the night melted away painfully. The light around the maternity hospital and the cool evening breeze painted a false picture of serenity. And though the night looked merry considering the beautiful structure that was the hospital, an overwhelming air of glumness draped the sick house.

Somewhere in the delivery room a woman lay between the thin thread that separated life from death. Remi had become emaciated due to long hours of spasmodic pains and torture. She looked frail and thoughtful. Mudi had to fight back his tears when he saw her. Her ravishing feature was now fading due to the throes of birth which she suffered.

Mudi was hurt because he could not physically assuage her pains or share in it. Yet, it was a burden for both of them. A burden of procreation which by nature women alone have to carry.

Pa Sunmonu had come around in the morning and was told not to disturb the patient. He was terribly disturbed. He could neither sit nor stand. Intense silence pervaded the hospital. Remi had to be sedated as blood and water were transfused into her body.

The doctor came out again and asked Mudi to go and pick up more things for the lady. Mudi was anxious to talk to someone. He needed soothing words from a concerned person to enliven his hope. The young man left the hospital with Nusi. He could not help admiring this lady's selflessness. She was one lady who did all things for him without being asked to. He cherished her friendship. But for Remi, Nusi would have been his wife.

"Do you think something will happen to her?"

He asked Nusi as soon as they were in the car.

"Remi will be alright. Most mothers suffer during their first childbirth," she replied reassuringly.

"I am afraid of this operation, you know she underwent surgical operation once," he added.

"It doesn't matter. Two operations cannot harm. I know of a man who has had four operations in seven years and he is still alive," remarked Nusi.

"Anyway man's life is in God's hand," concluded Mudi fatalistically.

"God will not harm good people, better be optimistic," she preached.

"I wish I could," replied the disturbed man.

It took Mudi a long time to finally persuade Nusi to take a rest for a few hours. He was touched by her care and deep concern. He felt he owed her a great deal. At least on this occasion he owed her his sanity. Nusi was indeed a friend.

Mudi was now left with his in-laws. Pa Sunmonu was already dozing in a corner. He pitied the old man. Moments like this were when parents' love for their children could be tested. Here was a man who drove out his daughter and even wished her doomed for marrying Mudi against his will.

"Is she alright now?" Mrs. Sunmonu asked, intruding upon Mudi's thoughts.

"Yes..." he answered, feeling disturbed. "And the baby." Mrs. Sunmonu went on.

"Will be delivered soon," Mudi replied, feeling irritated.

"Soon! How soon?" Remi's mother's tone was rising.

"Mama they will quarrel with you if you make noise here. The doctors are trying their best. You should pray for them like I am doing," Mudi said impatiently.

"But ... but," she stammered, not understanding the trend things were following.

The doctor came out and beckoned on Mudi. He ran to meet him. His movement woke Pa Sunmonu who had been snoring.

"She's woken up now. You can come to talk to her. She needs some soothing words. Meanwhile don't mention the operation while you talk," the doctor cautioned.

"No, I won't doctor. Thanks for everything." Mudi hurried into the room, his legs as light as feathers. The in-laws thought he would come to give them the news. When they saw him enter the room, they looked at each other and rose to the door. There was no one at the door, so they gained easy entrance.

"Daddy, you have come too!" Remi cried in her thin voice.

"Yes, my daughter. I am sorry for everything." Pa Sunmonu replied in a remorseful tone.

"I am happy now daddy. Even if I die I'll have no regrets, knowing that I have earned your forgiveness," she remarked.

"How can you talk of death now Remi. You'll give birth to this baby and the family will be united once again," her mother intervened.

"You'll bury us with big garments Remi as we did to our parents. That is the tradition. Don't talk of death, my daughter, it is an abomination," Pa Sunmonu cautioned in a weary voice. Mudi was immersed in the emotional outburst of the moment.

"Daddy, do you now accept Mudi as my legitimate husband?" she asked suddenly, taking them all by surprise.

"Why not?" Pa Sumonu replied. "After all if one does not put behind him past quarrels, he'll never find a playmate. My prayer now is that both of you should prosper and procreate in abundance."

"Thank you daddy I'll be indebted to you as long as I live." Mudi cut in, profuse in his gratitude.

"I'll be in peace forever now," Remi added.

"My daughter will..." Mrs. Sunmonu could not finish her statement because just then a nurse came to tell them that only one person should be with the patient at a time. The in-laws hesitatingly left the room for the couple.

"Darling to think we would experience this kind of warm acceptance was like a dream without substance at the beginning," Remi resumed when they were left alone.

"Yes, behind every unhappiness, there is a slight ray of hope that will be manifested only when the heart perseveres," Mudi replied philosophically.

"Hmm."

"We are enjoying these blessings now because we were hopeful," he added.

"Do you think we can go on being happy like this all our lives?" Remi asked.

"It depends."

"Can there be any loss if the whole of mankind should remain happy till eternity?"

"Happiness and sorrow are checks and balances for our behaviour. If we are not faced with some kind of misfortune in life we will never know the true value of joy."

"Will I survive this?" Remi asked, changing the pattern of discussion.

"What do you mean?" Mudi was confused, having been caught unawares by the question.

"The baby is dead and they are going to remove it. It will not be easy you know," she pointed out.

"Who told you that Remi?"

"I knew it and I feel it whenever the doctors talk."

"What you felt is untrue. The baby is not dead and there is not going to be any operation," he countered.

"I heard I have lost too much blood. And that is bad for me eh."

"Don't worry you will be alright. Everything has been taken care of."

"Whatever my parents do promise me you will harbour no hard feelings against them."

"The quarrel has been settled so don't talk of another one."

"You will always love them as you love me, Mudi."

"You know my heart, why do you talk like this?"

"I know you're afraid for me. But never mind since most things we fear are real."

"This type of talk is not good for your health."

"Alright promise me one thing and I'll stop talking."

"What is it?"

"Promise that you'll not renounce the world because of me."

"That can never happen. How can you think of being separated from me? What can equal sharing a blissful life with you?"

"Suppose I die."

"What do you mean?" Mudi was angry. "I will not listen to this kind of talk any more," he shouted.

"You like Nusi, don't you?" she continued.

"What's all this Remi?" Mudi asked getting infuriated with the way she talked.

"I approve of her. But promise that no matter what happens you will not grieve."

"And why should I grieve. Nothing will happen ... and please for your sake and mine forget this talk. It is unsettling."

Remi kept quiet.

At seven in the evening, the pain which had subsided for about six hours began again. The whole hospital was panic-stricken because of the suffering woman. A team of doctors converged to battle for the patient's life. It was a severe case, and everybody was prayerful. It was like one of those times when the spirit of death hovered around the operating table.

Around 9.00 p.m. there was a succession of baby cries. Consternated, everyone looked at the other. Hopes began to rekindle. But no one could exclaim in happiness yet. Mudi ran to the door and just then the cries stopped. He became jittery. He held on to the door knob. Then the baby cries came again. This time in an unorderly succession. It appeared the babies were two. Mudi's head was in the sky. He began dreaming, muttering the praise of his wife. He longed to hear her voice, to see smiles returning to her face and her enchanting beauty blooming once more. For two nights, Remi had suffered.

It was not until after about forty-five minutes that the door was opened. Everyone eager to hear the news rushed to the door. Remi's doctor, a bald headed man in his late fifties ignored the crowd and led Mudi to his office.

"Congratulations," he said unsmiling" your wife has put to bed two lovely babies, a boy and a girl."

Mudi was beside himself. "Oh thank you doctor, thank you, very much," he exclaimed. Suddenly he noticed the doctor's serious face.

"But wait a minute Dr. Johnson, what is the matter, what about Remi? What has happened to her? Where is my wife? Tell me doctor." He was agitated. The doctor walked over to him.

"That is rather unfortunate," he started. "Your wife was strong-willed. She held on for two nights. We tried but, she could not be saved."

Mudi's mind was amok. He felt his whole life had caved in. The doctor shook him. "The twins are there to show that all is not lost. It is difficult, but you must take grip of yourself."

"Promise that you'll not renounce the world because of me" ... "Suppose I die" ... "Promise that you will not grieve no matter what happens." These statements rushed back at Mudi, tormenting him. So these were statements from a dead woman. He felt this earlier but had dismissed it as an evil thought. It was as if his head had been set ablaze. He walked on, not feeling, not hearing, deeply submerged by the tragedy. The crowd caught up with him.

"What is the matter Mudi?" The awe-stricken voice of Mrs. Sunmonu cut through to him. He heard the lamenting voice of Pa Sunmonu rending the air.

"God of my ancestors, is this your promise?" Pa Sumonu cried. "Have you taken smiles from my face so soon?" He was hysterical. Mudi felt hands all over his body. Nusi held him ferociously and wept onto his chest. At that moment he felt like weeping. "Remi, dead?" he muttered. It was like he was asking himself. Suddenly there was pandemonium as Mrs. Sunmonu gave a strange mirthless laughter and fainted. She was revived instantly by doctors who rushed out.

Then slowly, the crowd in a mournful procession accompanied by intermittent emotional outbursts trooped out of the hospital. Mudi still kept a stone face. As the crowd melted away painfully like the night, he returned to the doctors. The night garb became darker and the light dimmer. It was a night of death with icy silence. A night of terror.

The Scars of the Moon

It was a long lonely night, quiet except for the chirping of nocturnal insects and the din of frogs from a nearby pond. The night was damp as there had been rain some four hours earlier. The grasses were moistened and the air freshened. The moon which had disappeared with the coming of the thunderstorm was already back at its beat, resuming its solitary stare. The orientation camp of the Youth Movement was draped with shadows of trees and of ghosts. The hostel blocks stood some 300 metres away from the camp clinic. Here over 4,000 Youth Marshals were undergoing a one-month paramilitary training in preparation for the national service. Lights from the dormitory cast silhouettes on the dark landscape which was only partially illuminated by the moonlight. The RSM Quarters where the general administration of the camp was carried out stood opposite the hostel from the eastern end of the camp gate. The only sign of life at the RSM Quarters was the lone soldier at the entrance. The black soldier stood erect like a statue and the glistening of lights on his soft beret cap created a mirage, an illusion of a dangling ghost.

Captain Audu Moses, Commander of Platoon 35 of the Youth Movement sat on a chair outside the living room serving as the camp clinic. A bottle of unfinished beer rested on a chair near him, but carefully positioned away from the movement of his legs. Light from the dangling cigarette on his lips glowed. Occasionally, he took a bite from the kolanut to ward off sleep. His tin of snuff, already emptied of its content laid at his feet. He had not bothered to pick it up out of annoyance that it had chosen such a night to finish. The interior of the one-room apartment serving as the clinic was well lit. The three fluorescent bulbs that graced the asbestos appeared too much for the medium-size room. The powerful electrical rays rather than enhancing the appeal of the clinic only advertised its poverty the more. The paints on the wall were already peeling off while the asbestos seemed ready to divulge its contents.

One long bench stood against the wall just by the entrance and a table and chair were at the right side of the room, overlooking one of the windows. As you came in through the door, the first thing you would notice was a spring bed, shielded now because of its present occupant. Since the commencement of the orientation exercise about three weeks ago, the clinic has not had an in-patient. Now a lone patient lay snoring on the cringing bed. A mere look at him should tell anyone he had gone through a riotous ordeal. A bloodstained bandage was woven round his head and his bruised lips held a bloody cotton wool. The patient was still dressed in the full attire of the Youth Marshal, which had been smeared with blood and mud. The room smelled of congealed blood and medicines, but the patient slept on.

The atmosphere in the clinic was silent. Agnes Temilade, one of the Youth Marshal doctors on duty tonight was leafing through her Bible. Her colleague, Omolola Omotunde, had tried unsuccessfully to engage her in talk, and had now given up. He decided to stroll out into the night.

"Hey, where are you going?" Agnes ventured when she saw him walking to the door.

"Out. I'm going for a walk. If you care you can join me," Omolola replied, trying to lure her out.

"The night is for demons to wander in. Men of God keep indoors at night," Agnes began, introducing one of her common religious admonitions.

"Only demons see demons at night," Omolola found himself replying. He knew she would feel insulted but he could not help it. He was surprised nevertheless with the look of terror in her eyes.

"May God save your soul," she hissed in a wicked tone.

Both of them sighed. Omolola shook his head and said within himself. "May God deliver you from yourself." He walked out. It was by sheer coincidence that both of them were on duty that night. The two were members of Platoon 35. It was strange for the two who had been drawn in an emotional battle to meet under the circumstance of the night when they had to keep vigil over a colleague who had gone berserk at the parade ground in the morning. Instead of the night drawing them together, it widened the gulf between them. Omolola doubted whether they would ever agree.

Stepping down from the raised platform onto the grass, he accosted Captain Moses who had just come back from behind the building where he had gone to ease himself. "Hi Captain, it's a long night," he greeted when they met.

"It's a terrible night my brother. I'm filled with a certain apprehension. I don't know why," the soldier replied.

"For Bitrus?" he asked looking towards the clinic's door for emphasis. He was surprised at the degree of emotion in Captain Moses' voice as he spoke.

"Yes for that poor boy, and for all of us," he said with unease, not knowing how to explain the gnawing emptiness he felt within him.

"How do you mean Captain?" Omolola asked, interested in knowing exactly what was disturbing the man he had come to see as an epitome of bravery.

Captain Moses shifted his position, and walked towards the chair. He sat heavily on the iron chair and took a sip from the bottle of beer. There was a look of worry in his eyes when he looked at the young doctor again. "I'm talking strange eh? Sometimes I talk like this. I do not know what is happening to me. Perhaps it is the effect of alcohol or lack of sleep. Alcohol can make us sober and our thinking dull," he said. "My brother," he resumed, "the night is not fit enough for any human activity, whatever it is," he added philosophically.

Omolola was amused. Captain Moses was obviously low. He did not want to catch the symptom too. The brief stay with Agnes inside the camp clinic was harrowing to him. He had to find his way out. "Well Captain, I think I should leave you with your thoughts. I'm going for a walk," he said and took off.

"My dear boy, don't go far. It is not a night to wander in," Captain Moses' voice followed him.

"I'll be alright," he replied just as Agnes came out singing a church hymn. "This church girl," he muttered as he walked on. "Now she'll begin to preach to Captain Moses about demons walking the wood at night."

Captain Moses' eyes strained from lack of sleep. He wiped his heavy eyelids and cursed under his breath. Why had the snuff chosen such a night to finish? His thought strayed to Bitrus and he felt a tinge of guilt.

Now he knew where his apprehension was directed. He was afraid something terrible would happen to the boy. That boy Bitrus, why? What had suddenly gone wrong with him? He had been such a nice boy. Captain Moses could not reconcile with the mental affliction the young chap was going through. He had hit the boy out of his ignorance. How could he have known that he had a mental problem? He had interpreted his unruly behaviour as an act of insubordination. He had been livid with rage and had descended savagely on the poor boy. Captain Moses was stricken with fear. He had seen the physical torture he inflicted on Bitrus as more inhuman than the skirmish caused by him at the parade ground in the morning. Captain Moses, in his naivety, had been provoked when Bitrus ran amok, tearing at the clothes of the female marshals, and caused such pandemonium that his platoon was in disarray. Not until the boy had been taken away before it dawned on him that he was mentally sick. The fact that all his actions were engineered by a reflex made him feel guilty and remorseful. He had been restless since the parade was dismissed. He had taken the night vigil assignment to himself to be sure the lad had cooled down before he could be transferred to a psychiatric hospital. The RSM had travelled to town and would not be back till the following day. He had to approve the transfer before anything could be done.

The night was wearing out itself slowly as the quietude deepened except with the little noises of night creatures. Captain Moses took another shot. It appeared as if his eyes were playing some puzzling tricks on him. The moon had some mystery about it, he thought. The clouds were not moving about it as before. It just stood there like a little balloon hanging in the space. Captain Moses imagined little children playing inside the moon. It was a strange play; they played with their legs up. They were walking on their heads. His eyes drooped with worry and they were watery. He felt cold within himself. Then he knew he had finally caught it. His dark past flashed back like an undesirable apparition. He knew he would finally catch it. Whenever he had the sour mood he remembered the incidents of his childhood which had kept haunting him. It was more turbulent for him during the first year of his marriage when his wife had threatened to divorce him if he did nothing about the hallucination. *The moon.* Captain Moses looked up at the heavenly object. *The moon caused it.* He trembled, and melancholy, like an electric wave, travelled through his veins. He wiped his watery eyes and took another sip from the bottle of beer. It was quiet all over. Agnes had stopped singing. She too appeared to be staring blankly at the vacant space and the moon. Captain Moses sighed. *We all have our moments of madness. That girl has some form of madness in her head. That's why she has renounced the world. I too, I had mine and that one who has wandered into the wood. The boy, Bitrus, has come to the end of the road. His own madness has ripened and had burst like a painful boil full of bitter pus.*

For an upward of nine months, Captain Moses had had no cause to keep a late night. He dreaded the night like the unseen jinn. *It is a strange night, this one,* he said to himself. *I have a phobia for the night as far back as I could remember. It has to do with my childhood affinity with the spirit world. I was supposed to be an outlaw of the spirit world, a kind of apostate or a prodigal. In my infant years, I had wandered into the night alone in my sleep, entered the recess of trees where we had a feast with gnomes. And thereafter, we had a wrestling in the open plain. We drank from the sap of trees to quench our thirst and roasted frogs, termites and nightingales for refreshment. It used to be a sweet festivity until my parents decided to sever my link with the spirit world.*

Though they succeeded with the help of a strong Boka from our village, my spirit companions still vowed never to leave me. The spirit father frequently visited me in my sleep, sometimes dressed as a poor beggar, sometimes as a nun, and sometimes as a farmer. Sometimes he would torment me and I would cry out from sleep, waking up the entire household. He stung like a scorpion and his venom was like that of a cobra. Sometimes when he came as a carpenter he would try to saw away at my limbs. For these physical tortures I usually woke up with terrific pains.

I hate the spirit father. I detest his diabolic attitude. I avoid anything that might bring me into contact with him. I do not go near trees at night, nor dare to cross a bush path. I do not fetch water from a well lest he pulls me down. I do not climb anything too high lest he dazzles me, make me feel dizzy and I fall headlong. But all these were in the past. I still have my nightmares though. The terror and fears of my childhood days had inflicted permanent scars on me. And I find myself oftentimes imagining gnomes walking about in the night and spirit children waiting to turn me into a playful doll. I hate the night for all its trauma and the nightmares. My wife, Mero, almost left me. How could I, a grown up, a soldier for that matter, be under the bondage of nightmares at this age?

The girl, Agnes moved and seemed to stare vacantly at Captain Moses who was lost in the maze of his own thoughts. She came down the platform steps, and started walking towards the hostel. Captain Moses did not look at her. He continued with his soliloquy.

I joined the army at the outbreak of the civil war to save myself from the affliction of my past. By confronting the fear itself, I had thought of banishing all traces of it. I took up soldiering as an act of rebellion, to spite my spirit companions and revolt against their slavery. It was not easy those first years. But fear was rampant then as death itself. Fear of perdition, decapitation and annihilation. Fear was the commonest companion not to be acknowledged. It was always there. Our Battallion Commander used to tell us. Our Battalion Commander was a lion at the battlefield. He used to tell us. 'This is a battle of nerves. The cowards don't survive this kind of war. The weak and the cowardly die first. So, banish your fears and face death with a stubborn will.' I saw fighting then as my own battle of survival. I never questioned the reason for the mass killing, sacking of villages, ravaging of properties, looting and raping we did as soldiers. I was concerned with my own liberation. Every bullet I fired, every house I razed, every rebel I shot were all towards one purpose, the annihilation of my own innate rebel, fear. I failed to realise that one is supposed to master his fear and learn to control it. You cannot rout fear; fear is an integral part of our life.

Somewhere in the wood, Omolola emerged at an open glade. Here the grass was rich and tough. The grass made funny little noises as Omolola's canvas shoes trod on them. The moon shone even brighter now and it glistened on the shining edges of the grasses. Unhindered, the young doctor went on. Rodents were free and had come out to play in the grass. They hurried off whenever they encountered the tall form of the intruder. Omolola could feel the whispering course of a stream nearby. Upon an instinct, he decided to see the water flow and he changed direction to where the clean water flowed from. The gentle wind from the trees around the stream was serene and satiating. Light animals jumped from tree to tree in a form of nocturnal game. The moon had abandoned the open grass and it now peeped between openings among the leaves. The young man stooped and took the water with both hands. The water was cool on his palms. He splashed the liquid of life on his face. He washed his face three times as if carrying out a ritual bath. There was a rush of wind now and the leaves billowed. The moon came out full blown as if making a testimony, and reflected on the surface of the water.

Omolola watched the beautiful reflection. The surface of the stream glittered with silver linings and the smooth waves appeared to transport the light. Omolola stared: *if only the world could be as peaceful and free as this little stream. If only we could live our lives unencumbered by life's travails. If only we could live free like the moon up there ... he thought and stood up. The whole gamut of life began to spin out a new meaning to him. But the moon is also not free with the clouds and thunder-storm lording over it. Sometimes the moon has to abandon the sky when the sun comes calling. Perhaps we are never really born free,* he reasoned. *Perhaps we could never be free. Perhaps...*

Omolola thought of Bitrus and his affliction and thought why a bright young chap like him should carry such a burden. Bitrus had been such a charming and easy-going youth marshal, a darling of most ladies in the platoon. But fate has a way of playing its cold trick on human beings. Even if Bitrus finally got well, how would he get over the trauma of the public disgrace his mental affliction had caused him? he thought. The young man looked at the ageing night. The moon now looked like a small bowl on a vast ocean while the clouds now moving eastward swept over the bowl-like moon in the tide. Omolola's mind conjured the picture of a corpse in the funeral pyre. He moved away from the stream and sat on an anthill. The top was still moist from the earlier rain. He stood up and started walking towards the opposite direction. Omolola was not aware of a pair of eyes prying on his thoughts from the top of a tree. He walked on and stopped about 500 metres from the stream and rested on the trunk of a tree.

Omolola stared at the beautiful reflection of the lambent moon. He could still hear the slow murmuring of the stream and the little noises of the insects. He felt at peace with himself and the world. It was as if he had broken free from a certain shackle. He began to dream of life after the Orientation Camp. What did the outside world have in store for them? He did not know. But it would be good to be free once again. The idea of freedom thrilled him. He picked a fallen leaf and began to fold it. He was just folding it without really having anything in mind to do with it. His thoughts began to flow, and his wet lips moved as if he was talking to some unseen being around.

In another one week, he thought, *we should be out of this enclave called the Youth Orientation Camp and I'll be free to carry out my professional obligation as we swore at the School of Medicine. At first it was fun. But the tedious morning drill, the evening exercise, the long trek in the jungle, the paramilitary training had sought to make robots out of us.*

I have never envied or admired soldiers beyond the beauty of their uniform. The violence which they unleashed on the civilian populace had made me to abhor them. I have never come so close to soldiers until I came to the orientation camp. I always view them with terror as they club down motorists, crackdown on exuberant university students or loot the wares of market women.

I have never come so close to a soldier like Captain Audu Moses. He is a perfect gentleman. Captain Moses. It is his sense of humour that endeared him to us. He is an expert when it comes to entertainment. Because our platoon was quite homely and lively, many considered ours as the laziest platoon but it never bothered us. Captain Moses took special interest in me, because according to him, I look like somebody from his childhood. I often avoided him at the parade ground because of my deficiency in carrying out the military drill. I often stayed in the rear away from reach. But Captain Moses would bring me out. He takes delight in seeing my faitering steps.

I had to turn my deficiency into humour. So, whenever I am called to act, it is always time for laughter.

Ah, Agnes, that's a girl after my heart. Why did I choose to fall in love with her? It was a matter of coincidence, though. An accident had brought us together. I had knocked her down inadvertently during one of our morning drills, having carried out wrongly the instruction of the platoon commander. Out of guilt I decided to visit her at the hostel in the evening to see how she was recuperating. I felt uneasy for hurting her. I was doing all I could to assuage her pains. The accident made us intimate and I found myself drawn towards her and she began to appear in my dream.

At last when I spoke to her about my love for her she began to shun me, even going to the extent of being bitter. To Agnes, I was yet to be delivered from worldly bondage. She said I was a slave of the world, that I needed to be liberated and find solace in the Lord. Sometimes I hate Agnes and I feel like hurting her. I feel like doing something terrible to her for toying with my heart's desire.

Agnes has declared war on the world, relinquishing the beauty and keeping affinity with the dirty and the unkempt. You need to see the extent of savagery Agnes has committed against her beauty. She hates adornment of any sort and leaves her hair, once in shining strands dishevelled. Her sensuous lips now crack due to severe denial and mental torture.

I could have forgotten about Agnes and the heartache she has caused me. That could have been a better option, instead of allowing her to drag me out of the world I know into the *unfathomable uncertainties of her own, or make me uncomfortable in my own little world. I could have simply done that but the more I see Agnes, the more the hatred I feel for her, the more the tenderness I want to show to her.*

Why they decided to bring us together this night, I do not know. The brief stay with her inside that cubicle they call the camp clinic was terrorising to me. The girl appeared to be enjoying herself while I mooned away.

A tree fell somewhere. There was a rush of wind, then a strange laughter downstream. His thought flow was broken. Omolola was afraid. The laughter was so strange. It was as if an intruder had been spying on him. It was a mysterious laughter, strange and unnatural. Omolola felt his lung thickening and his breathing impaired. There was a cold electric sensation running down his spine. He waited but the laughter never came back. Then he heard the shuffling of a human feet in a disappearing act, marching roughly on leaves and twigs of trees and he beat a quick retreat.

Omolola ran. He had never been so shaken. Could the laughter have come from a human being or an ape? It was so unnatural but familiar. He felt a gnawing sadness flowing from his bowel? What an unnatural spectacle for a beautiful night! He felt apprehensive. Had he met a gnome? What could have happened? Then he remembered Agnes' warning about the demon. Did he encounter a demon? *No, it's impossible*, he told himself. *We have outlived the world of demons and vampires. We are in a modern world of jets and rockets. Those pictures of demons in films are simply imitations of our dark past.*

By the time Omolola began to see the familiar lights of the clinic and the hostels from afar, he knew he had reached safety. His fear was gone. If he told Agnes about the mysterious laughter, she would only laugh at him. He decided to forget the experience.

Just then a figure loomed before him. It was Agnes. Omolola reduced his pace to see the direction of her walk. But she was coming in his direction. Where could she be going? Perhaps she was going to look for him. Agnes looked cherubic in the vast moonlight. Her skirt billowed in the free night breeze. She had removed her scarf and her hair flowed freely now. She looked like the reincarnation of another being.

Omolola smiled when she came a few metres abreast of him. He did not see a return of the smile but something sparkled in Agnes' eyes.

"Hi," Omolola greeted when they met. "So, you've decided to take the air too. Or are you out to look for me?" he asked.

"What for?" Agnes asked, her combative posture surging up. She was still beautiful in her present posture, making whatever she said appear a farce.

"Well, out of concern."

"What have you been doing in the forest, walking about like a spirit?" she asked with venom in her voice.

"Sorry dear, I know you'll be lonely without me," he teased her and tried to pat her shoulder but she backed off. Omolola smiled and caught her by the hand. He made her to face him. Both of them were panting now.

"Sometimes you make me hate you. Why? Aren't you a woman?" Omolola asked, his mouth filled with bitter saliva. He shook her.

"Leave me alone," she jerked off her hand. "I hate you, I hate you... " and she broke down. Omolola attempted to soothe her, but she broke free and ran off.

She cried. Agnes cried. "What could be tormenting her"? he reflected. "Perhaps it is the moon," he said. "The moon has a way of influencing us." He stared at the vacant face of the moon. As he walked towards the moon, it walked towards him too till it fell behind the RSM Quarters.

A Gamble With Life

When my friend's father, Mr. Agbaje, left for work in the morning I decided to put my plan into action. I must abscond before he returned in the afternoon, I decided. So, when my friend, Seni, approached me to go with him on our daily routine of picking mangoes and pears, I declined, saying that I had a stomach upset. I discerned from his face that he was not happy with this. Probably he was thinking I had started thinking bad of him too and planning to back out. I gave no conscience to this thought. I simply wanted to leave.

After he had left, I put on my trousers and packed my few possessions into my schoolbag. I hurriedly scribbled a note, telling my friend I had left for school. I tip-toed through the backyard like a juvenile about to commit a larceny. My heart was pounding in my head. If I should be caught...

If anyone should see me escaping he would simply label me the guilty one. When I succeeded in getting away from the compound, I uttered a silent prayer of thanks.

I joined the teeming crew of Lagos folks. People were trooping out ceaselessly from every corner. Serious-minded people and the crooks; they all mingled in the early morning rush that was typical of Lagos life. There were the poor and the rich. We lived in the poor quarters of the city. Our house was a small oven-like structure made of iron sheets. The house had become crude black with smoke because it served both as the living room as well as the kitchen. Mr. Agbaje lived alone until I and my friend joined him. He was a clerk with the Railway.

There were many things I had to run away for in that house, I said to myself. I thanked God I was successful in my flight. I took my place in the crowd waiting for the *molue*. Soon they came and the air became frenzy with the conductors shouting the names of their routes and the passengers bracing up for the struggle to secure seats. The *molue* never really stopped. And as I made a leap to catch the hang-on at the door, the driver accelerated. I yelled as I faltered but a man quickly got hold of my hand and flung me inside.

I hurt my side against the sharp edge of a seat. I moaned and the passengers began to talk.

"You're lucky young chap. Next time, be faster. Boys younger than you have learnt to leap like a monkey. Are you new in the city?" a man asked arrogantly.

"Thank God we're saved another obituary case. Last year a schoolboy fell out when a *molue* was in motion and he died instantly," a market woman added.

Her statement sent a chill of fear through my spine. They talked of death as if the schoolboy actually wished to die. No one blamed the driver. I continued to rub my side, not minding their unsympathetic talk. Soon I was lost in the midst of the passengers. There was nowhere to move and no pure air to breath. I paid ten kobo to the conductor when he got to me.

"You're the boy who wanted to die eh?" he asked sarcastically. "Why don't you go and take a leap from the coconut tree in your village?" He was huge and fierce looking, so, I had no wish to even bat him an eyelid. I uttered my prayers again as I jumped down from the *molue* at the last bus stop. I examined my wound, it was not much. A sharp iron had cut my shirt and pierced through my skin. I hurried into the main building of the railway station. Many people were outside, waiting for their luggage to be weighed. I climbed into one of the coaches reserved for the journey up-north. Selling of the tickets had not yet commenced. That was my plan to come early so as to escape paying for the ticket. Infact, I had no money on me.

I got myself ensconced beside a window. The squirming of the worms in my stomach reminded me that it was since yesterday afternoon that I ate food last. Yes, yesterday I regretted following Seni to Lagos. It was the event of yesterday that made me to flee the house.

Seni and I attended the same school. We were also classmates and friends. It was at the middle of the third term when we had the mid-term break. I did not want to go home so as not to meet my uncle with whom I had a quarrel before leaving. I did not want to go home until the end of the session when I would go to Benin to see my parents. I started thinking of how to spend the one week break. I was still unable to get out of this dilemma when Seni approached me. He said we could go to Lagos together to spend the holiday. I was glad at the suggestion because I loved adventure. I quickly volunteered everything I had and that evening we boarded a

Lagos-bound train.

While on the train, Seni lectured me on what to tell his father on arrival in Lagos. He said I should tell him I had a brother working with the Ministry of Works and living at Alagogo Meji. The two of us would go out immediately we arrived at their house to look for my brother and we would come back after some time saying that my brother had travelled to Minna on official assignment and would not be back until after two weeks. Thus, I would be able to stay in their house for a week unquestioned. I did not like this idea. He did not tell me earlier we had to lie before I could be accepted into their family. After some arguments I agreed with the plan.

We arrived Lagos the following day in the afternoon. We met Seni's father who listened to my tale and told us to go in search of my brother immediately. We went and came back. But he was not in when we came. There was nothing available to eat and there was nothing more on us. Seni decided that we should go to pick mangoes and pears. His father did not come back until nightfall and immediately he came, he went straight to bed. Before we could wake up in the morning he had gone again. We began to live on picking fruits at the Railway Quarters.

I grew annoyed with my friend because he did not tell me he was bringing me to Lagos to suffer. I started wondering also if Mr. Agbaje was actually the father of my friend. I threw this question of neglect at my friend and he told me his father was a mean man. He spent money on himself only; that was why he kept late night. He told me the man had sent away his mother because he did not want anyone to alter his patterned life. He had only three children and two of them lived with the wife. Seni told me he had gone there once but the man came to take him back to Lagos. He had even threatened him with stopping the payment of his school fees if he should go there afterwards.

Four days after our arrival, Seni suddenly came up with some money. He did not tell me who gave him the money and I did not persist when he said I should not worry. I had no idea he had stolen the money from his father. He had discovered that the man was not actually poor as he pretended to be. He had helped himself with some money from his box. Seni took me to a *buka* where he declared a feast. From there we proceeded to the Bar Beach where we spent the rest of the money on gambling and suya. To us that was our best day of the holiday.

I was surprised the following day when we woke up with virtually nothing to spend. I began to suspect my friend. Why spending the money in haste when we still had more days before the end of the holiday? I asked myself. My suspicion was confirmed when Mr. Agbaje came home in the afternoon. He had come to collect the money he left in his box. The money was not complete so, he called the two of us for interrogation. I stared at my friend but he averted his eyes. The angry shout of Mr. Agbaje brought some people to the house. A man said he saw us at a *buka* the previous day and concluded that we could have stolen the money. The two of us were spellbound. Seni looked at me and I stared back at him. We had been caught, there was no point denying the charge as we could be followed to the *buka* and the food seller would recognise us. None of us spoke. We just looked on.

"Seni tell us who gave you the money you took to the buka?" Mr. Agbaje asked his son.

"My friend's brother gave us the money," Seni lied.

"But you said his brother was not in town," Mr. Agbaje countered. He looked at me angrily. I averted my gaze. I was terribly angry with Seni. He was making me look like a fool. He told me to say my brother had travelled when indeed I had no brother in Lagos. Now he was saying that my brother had given the money which I did not know its origin. Mr. Agbaje decided to follow us to Alagogo Meji to confirm.

"Sir, he has no brother at Alagogo Meji; it's only a... " began Seni.

"So, you have both been playing dirty tricks on me. Come on, tell me the whole lot of it, dirty swine," he ordered angrily. I wanted to tell him that I knew nothing about it. That Seni had not told me right from school that we would tell any lie. He did not inform me how he got the money too. But upon instinct. I decided to remain silent.

"It must be that boy, don't mind the innocent look on his face," said Abefele. Abefele was a jovial man who had taken special interest in me since we arrived. He always asked me consolatively if I had got any news about my brother to which I would reply promptly. His sudden outburst surprised me.

"He's a cheat; see how he fooled all of us into believing that he had a brother here. He must have pushed Seni into stealing the money," he added.

"No, no, believe me, I know nothing about this. He invited me. I know nothing about the money," I pleaded.

"Shut up brute! I should take you to the police-station. You'll be taught that stealing and lying are crimes," Mr. Agbaje shouted at me.

I bit my finger in regret. Seni did not even utter a statement to absolve me of this blame. People begged Mr. Agbaje not to take me to the police-station as he threatened. He then decided that he would follow us to the school to report the matter to our Principal. Seni was severely punished but nothing was done to me. I knew my evil day was just being postponed. Somehow I felt no pity for Mr. Agbaje. That was the best punishment for a miser, I decided. But I hated Seni for refusing to exonerate me. I decided there and then that I had had enough.

The coach was beginning to get full now. I began to feel dizzy. I did not want to beg. Then I decided that to get something to eat I would make friends with any student I meet on the train. Probably I would get one to buy me food. I took out my *Incorruptible Judge* and began to scan blindly through it. I fell asleep in the process and the train had started to move by the time I woke up. There was a man sitting beside me. His face was buried in a big newspaper and two other women were sitting opposite me.

I began to feel hungry again. I peeped out through the window. I began to dream of lion and elephant as the train travelled through the rain forest of the south. The landscape was rich and deep green in colour. The approaching sound of the ticket collector woke me up from my day-dream. I leapt up from my seat and nearly stepped on a baby playing on the train alley. I ran into the toilet and bolted the door. I bore my suffering silently waiting for the man to move on. But he did not. Instead he stopped at the toilet and decided to see if anyone was inside. He called but I refused to answer. Sensing that someone was inside he became angry and applied pressure on the door till I could no more resist. He forced the door open and pulled me out. He slapped and kicked me. I ducked and fled. He gave a chase. There was pandemonium in the train as some were hailing me and others were shouting thief! He caught me at the third coach where another ticket collector blocked my way. He took me by the collar and dragged me on to the coach where he stopped checking. People trailed behind us to see what would happen to me. They began to talk.

"Perhaps he's a runaway. I know of one in my compound. He'll disappear for weeks, putting his parents in panic," a man said.

"He could be one of those rogues who board the train to rob

people. So small a boy, trying to dodge paying for the ticket. He should be taught an unforgettable lesson," another man added.

"Poor boy, have pity on him. Who knows may be he has no one to take care of him. Where are you going young boy?" an old woman asked.

I was not allowed to answer as a man intervened.

"See how well dressed he is. Who says this one has no one to care for him? Officer take him away. He must pay for the ticket. Let him pawn one of those materials he put on if he can't get the money."

"Now I have to deliver you to the railway policemen at the next station unless you pay up," the ticket man threatened.

I did not say a word because I knew my fate was no longer in my hand. Just then a man stood up. It was the man sitting next to me. He was a strange kind of man. People looked strangely at him too. He wore a white shirt, white knicker and a beret cap. What made him look odd was because he had no shoe on.

"Officer leave the boy alone. I'll pay for his ticket," he offered and gave the man a new five naira note. I was spellbound and knew not what to do. The ticket man wrote the receipt, gave it to me and returned the change to the man. He was asked to give it to me. Everyone was surprised. The man had not spoken since the beginning of the trip. No one knew his identity. They began to talk silently about him. The ticket collector looked at me in an unfriendly manner and said: "You're saved this time but don't try to be smart next time. You might be unlucky." I told myself that I did not need his advice. I had already advised myself.

I returned to my seat and thanked the man profusely for helping me out. He told me not to worry. At the next station he bought food and we ate. I began to feel the mercy of God which was often manifested through human beings. He told me he was formerly a school teacher and that he left because he did not like the job. He told me he was now a businessman. He talked to me about so many things till I began to feel sleepy. Because of yesterday's incident I did not have sufficient sleep. Now nature was demanding its due. The man understood this and stood up. He told me he was going to the door to enjoy the breeze. I was grateful for the opportunity to sleep conveniently.

In my sleep I dreamt of so many incomprehensible things. I woke up with a light headache. New people now sat opposite me. I looked for my canvas shoe, it was gone. My schoolbag was also nowhere to be found. I began to get frightened. I went to the door of the coach. The man was not there. I went from coach to coach, there was no one like him anywhere. I started lamenting. People blamed me for being careless. I did not think he could take away my belongings. He was so nice; no it could not be him, I decided. Someone advised me not to get down at my destination that I should follow the train a station ahead of where I would stop. He told me that the man would assume I had gotten down and then he would feel free.

The man's advice was proved right because as we went past my station, the man came out of hiding. I saw him carrying my canvas shoe. He also carried his possessions in my schoolbag. I was enraged and at the same time afraid. I informed the people in my coach and some grown-up men followed me. As the man saw me approaching with the men, he took to his heels. We pursued and other people joined. He was stopped at the adjoining coach and people began to beat him. I felt pity and hatred for him. I was puzzled by this act. My property was recovered and he was handed over to the railway police as we got to the next station.

On my way back to the school, I thought how strange people could be. Here was a man who appeared as an angel but was actually a devil in sheep's clothing. The fact that he paid my train fare confused my thought about him. I thought of Mr. Agbaje too who had no feeling for his son. The thought of Mr. Agbaje brought back my forgotten fear. I prayed silently he should not turn up at our school. Innocence had been given a bad name and no one would likely believe me. Only one person, Seni could bring me out of this. If he refused to say the truth I vowed I would hate him forever. I had in fact gambled with life and I knew what I was experiencing now was the music.

Ordinance of Love

Many had wondered how Hamida had come to combine beauty with humility. Perhaps her brilliant academic career had created for her a picture of awe and respect. Hamida was a promising first class candidate in the Department of Sociology at the university, and many students aware of her charm and excellent record revered her. Many also considered her unapproachable for love talks because of her detached emotional built. She and Ansi viewed each other with some form of sacredness, and related with an aloofness common among great minds not wishing to concede superiority to each other. It was expected that the two would break record by clinching the coveted first class honours. The department had not produced any since the inception of the university.

It was the expatriate lecturer, Dr William Keith that first brought them together. He had invited the bewildered students to his office one afternoon to rub minds. He had told the two of them that they needed to work together for they would be a great gift to their country just emerging from the euphoria of independence from the British. Dr Keith noted that he had observed a gulf between them, and advised that as students of sociology they needed to show humanity a path to redemption. According to him, human beings have, through technology, conquered the space and by day had continued to bring the stars, the moon and other planets nearer to the earth but have not yet learnt how to live harmoniously with each other as one family under God. "We wake up each day with a renewed determination to continue the extermination of the human race," he had said.

The nation at the time of Dr Keith's observation was truly going through a post-natal labour due to bickerings among those who liberated it. Unlike the others, the country came out of the tutelage of colonial serfdom without wounds or scars. But the nationalists who had cooperated to drive away the colonial overlords had retreated to their respective ethnic courtyards where they fanned the embers of tribal acrimony. The nation's fragile unity was threatened and there were general unease and rancour everywhere.

The campuses were not insulated from the malaise. University authorities had banned tribal groupings and associations but they continued to flourish, undeterred.

Dr Keith had concluded that both of them would make a remarkable pair should they decide to marry. It was a statement they both responded to with an astounding laughter and disbelief. None of them had thought the lecturer harboured such a strong emotional feelings about them. Dr Keith was a divorcee with two grown-up children back home in Pensylvania, and had considered his Sociology class a part of his family and kin. Hamida and Ansi, concluded that Dr Keith was a likeable fellow and they soon found themselves going together for a chat with their new-found friend. But the two remained aloof from each other emotionally. Their relationship wore on with a strange formal tone. Hamida was the first to succumb, having discovered that they both operated at a psychic equilibrium. She fantasised on a blissful future with Ansi as his wife. But she was surprised that each time she tried to get intimate Ansi would withdraw into a protective shell. She was never daunted as she fought her battle of recognition. Hamida was aware of the cynical laughter of the desperado students but she paid no attention to them. She clung stubbornly to Ansi like the last twig caught by a drowning swimmer. Hamida remained comforted by the exhilarating feelings of inner peace which she felt in the presence of Ansi.

Then one day Ansi had called on her at Nana Hall looking depressed and forlorn as a weather-beaten strand. He had come to seek her help in a matter that had constituted a heartache to him. Ansi was in love with a 300 level student in the Department of Modern European Languages. Hamida's face was flushed with disappointment. She was sad and her voice shook from a psychological disorientation.

"What's wrong with you Hamida? You look so sad. Are you unhappy that I'm falling in love? No, you've never acted like this before. I thought you're always happy with whatever I do." Ansi ranted, feeling quite uneasy with the depressed mood of his partner.

"Sorry about my mood," Hamida pleaded. "I'm not feeling too fine. Please let's talk about this some other time," she advised. Ansi went back to the hostel disappointed. He felt bereaved. His only friend and confidant seemed to have deserted him.

Hamida cried all night when she got to her room. Her friend,

Fati, was worried for her. She became angry and thought of Ansi as a selfish and sadistic individual. Why did he encourage the poor girl only to ditch her?

"Leave Ansi alone Fati, it's my fault. I encouraged him. He tried to dissuade me but I refused," Hamida begged when Fati threatened to challenge Ansi the next day.

"Who is he, Hamida to look down on you like that? It's of no use, wallahi my friend, to cry your heart out for someone who does not care," Fati thundered in annoyance.

"Help me Fati, what can I do? I feel so dejected. I won't be able to go to class tomorrow in this state," Hamida pleaded clinging to her friend for solace.

"Well someone has to talk to him. But if you'll take my opinion, Hamida, I'll ask you to ignore him. It's of no use. Most men are self-centered and crude," contributed Fati who had been jilted thrice.

"I can't Fati. It's not easy with this thing you know. It's been my fault, I know. I worked up myself unnecessarily. But I never knew it would come to this," she wept afresh. Fati suggested she took valium to relieve her of a long night of torture and anguish. Hamida soon drifted into a fitful nightmare.

In her sleep, she dreamt that she and Fati were returning from the birthday party of a friend in Kabuga when the storm began to rage and the elements became tensed with suppressed passion. They started off, running to make it to shelter before the rains would be let loose. Her bag fell off as she was running, and she shouted at Fati to wait so that she could collect the bag but she did not. Hamida ran after the bag which had been blown off by the wind. She ran until she got to a ditch where it had landed. She went into the ditch. As she stooped to pick the bag, surprisingly it turned into a monster. Hamida shouted, and turned to bolt. The monster caught her by the hand and whispered. "It's me darling, why do you cry so?" She screamed and woke with a start.

"Wake up Hamida, wake up! What's that noise about?" her room-mate, shook her.

Hamida's heart raced in palpitation as she dragged herself up from the wearied bed. "Sorry Fati, it's been a dream. I had a nightmare. Sorry about that," she apologised, yawning at the same time. Hamida felt a dull ache in her head. Her head appeared to be swimming in the blues. The light had gone off, so she was perspiring heavily.

"Wallahi Hamida, I tell you, take it easy with this thing. Don't break yourself down because of Ansi," her room-mate advised.

Hamida felt sorry for herself. Her sleep had been rewarded with headache and gnawing pains in her joints. She decided she would skip the class that day. Hamida returned to sleep after she had a shower. The poor girl had been casual with the treatment of love advances before now. Hamida, before now, had treated with detachment men's advances, including that of the customs officer, Tomboiya her mum's favourite. Tomboiya had been helping her mum whenever she was passing through the Malam Aminu Kano International Airport on her business trips to Saudi Arabia. Hamida never liked him and the other two Tilde and Hadi who had been pestering her. Ansi's was Hamida's first experience of genuine love. Hamida decided that love, perhaps, had no rewards but pain and misery. Why had the love for Ansi almost wrecked her? She had depreciated emotionally within the past few hours.

It was Fati who met Ansi the next day when he came and told him Hamida was ill. He left a note, promising to check the next day. It was however not until the following Thursday that he saw her. Ansi was surprised to see how lean and withdrawn she had become. By then Hamida had developed a coping strategy for her psychological trauma. She had resolved to accept defeat in love. It was a difficult decision though. Hamida decided to put her faith in Allah and to help Ansi as much as she could to realise his love ambition. Ansi felt sorry but was amazed at the energetic zeal with which Hamida pursued his strives for Kemi's love. Kemi had been unmoved and cynical about Ansi's love advances, but Hamida's involvement thawed her hardened mind. She eventually saw Hamida as a caring, selfless and loving person. The speed at which their relationship grew surprised the Yoruba girl who had earlier joined others in labelling Hamida a proud self-centered personality.

* * * * * *

Soon afterwards, Ansi came to Nana Hall to invite her to a movie. Kemi had travelled downsouth and would not return to the campus until the next week. Hamida was happy with another opportunity to get close to Ansi, just in case.

"Have you seen this before?" Ansi asked her as they stood at The Cinema. "It is *The Travesty of Justice*, a film adaptation of the novel by Geraldine Melvin," he explained.

"Ah, that British novelist," Hamida contributed.

"Yes. There is a recurrent motif of poverty and its unpleasant consequences in Melvin's stories."

"I have read one of his novels, *The Holy Sinner*, but not *The Travesty of Justice*," she said.

"The poor always lose is the common theme in Melvin's novels. It is the same with *The Travesty of Justice* which bemoans the futility of justice. The law decides. Whether the decision is right or wrong, justice is based on proof. Whoever has proof gets the favourable judgement. In this novel, an innocent man was implicated in a murder case but all proofs and evidences were against him. So, while the criminal escaped untried, the innocent man was sentenced to death."

"Hm... a very pathetic story," contributed Hamida.

"It's very tragic," noted Ansi.

"You know something like that was reported in the media recently. A man was arraigned before a tribunal on a charge of armed robbery. He was found guilty and shot by a firing squad. But his family, convinced of his innocence went to court, and the slain man was eventually found innocent. The court ruled that compensation be paid to the slain man's family," Hamida explained.

The movie gave them a spiritual lift. It was another opportunity for the soulmates to get together. Escorting her back to the hostel that night, Ansi caught her by the hand and whispered "Hamida, you're very interesting to talk to."

"Hm... a nice thing to hear. I never realised that," she said avoiding his eyes.

"Honestly, I mean it. I don't know the kind of feeling I have when I'm with you. You're just too understanding. I don't know what I can do without you."

"Well, what are friends for, come to me whenever you have something to talk about. I appreciate the sentiments," replied the lady. Sometimes a man or woman with a heavy heart wants to cry. He or she might need someone to give a helping hand, or a shoulder to weep on. Every man needs someone to unburden his heart to, someone who understands.

* * * * * *

Hamida was thrilled when at the end of the semester, Ansi

dropped by on his way to his village. Hamida lived in a new building with her mother. Ansi was surprised at the opulence in which she lived, as she never discussed her parental background with him. He learnt that she was orphaned and she lived with her widowed mother who also had an estate in Zauda. Mother and daughter were happy to receive him. They were both extravagant in entertaining him. Hamida's mum had thought it was her daughter's fiance on a visit. They wanted him to spend the night but he had decided against it. Ansi felt uncomfortable with their care and his mind became torn between love for Kemi and the intimate affection for Hamida. Ansi felt disoriented. He had tried to avoid this kind of emotional scene. But Hamida had been such a fantastic friend and he always found himself trying to please her as much as he could.

A sullen Hamida was cheered up when Ansi invited her on a visit to his village before the end of the semester holiday. Ansi regretted not staying for the night as events later unfolded. He was in the driver's side of the 14-seater Urvan bus taking them to Dakata. He cast appreciating glances at the beautiful landscape and the Sahel savannah of the north. He was marvelling at the sights and daydreaming. Some few kilometres more they would be at Adok. After Adok they would still have to pass through Donawa and Zulma before arriving at Dakata. He was wondering about the tales of internecine wars that had taken place between the Donawans and the Dakatas, his people. He was thinking of the long distance between the two and wondered how they risked going to war with one another. But war was part of life in those days. Kingdoms grew from wars of conquest and armies were built from captives of battles. Ansi was thinking about how man had perfected the skill of warfare and made more enmity between nations and states.

The blasting of a car's horn interrupted his thought. The driver of the Urvan bus gave way, cursing "*Dan banza*. Go and meet your mother in the grave." A man unhurriedly hoofed by on his donkey and Ansi was amused at the way the man and the animal made it on to their destination. Then it happened. A few kilometres away from the billboard marked: *Welcome to Dakata, the home of Bamari drinks,* a chain of vehicles lined up and brought the traffic to a temporary halt. Many of the passengers and the drivers had alighted and were partaking in the struggle to extricate a man from a trapped car. The man was the one who overtook them in a grey-coloured 504 car.

Casualties numbered three. The driver of the trailer and the 911 lorry escaped unhurt, but the two men riding monkey on the back of the lorry died instantly for they came down with their heads. The mangled remains of the driver who overtook them was brought out. The middle-aged man was gasping for breath and blood was oozing from his nose. He fainted and sympathisers applied several breath-resuscitating measures to revive him. He gave up not quite three minutes after. Women cried and men shook their heads, gnashing their teeth at the overpowering effect of death over human life. A bearded grey-haired man who had been counting his rosary with deep-seated concentration whispered *inna lilahi wahina ilaai rajihuna*. The crowd broke up and everyone returned to their vehicles. Somewhere an owl cried and a dog howled in a nearby village. Most of the drivers were cowed by the horror while some hardened ones sped away, scowling at the slowing ones to give way.

They sped away causing more pandemonium with their blasting horn. To them misfortune must not slow down the business of livelihood. Ansi wished he had stayed the night at Hamida's place. It was dusk when he arrived at Dakata.

* * * * * * *

Hamida's visit to Dakata coincided with the night of the *Kemgbe* dance, the eve of the wedding of Salimata, Ansi's cousin. It was a festive time in the village. The dance normally was held under the big *Odan* tree at the village square. It was the usual rendezvous for the young unmarried boys and girls, where future matrimonial deals were often sealed.

That night the atmosphere was serene and the moon suspended above and centering the arena was like a lustral gold on a magnificent umbrella and the stars like multihued bulbs adorning a pavilion. To Hamida, the moon shone overwhelmingly like an imperial lantern showering sparkling lights on people's mien. The palm trees rustled from the gentle tilt of the wind. Hamida and Ansi squatted on an uncompleted building overlooking the centre of the dance.

Two girls were beating the gourd with their palms while the third beat an accompanying tune with a short stick. The lead singer, Kulu, and six other dancers sang soulful tunes that reverberated through the quietness of the night. An old woman, Nma, patron of the maids, squatted on a low stool staring at the young dancers with nostalgic amusement.

Now the lead singer had introduced a melodic tune, taking occasional leaps and the beat on the gourd became ecstatic. The crowd clapped with euphoric enjoyment. She started a song:

> *My teeming charming compatriots,*
> *Flowers of the village harem,*
> *Daughters of the beautiful moon,*
> *I plead with you on my knees*
> *To entreat my old granny*
> *Not to pawn me to the bicycle repairer.*
> *The bicycle repairer is a mean man*
> *The bicycle repairer is a greedy old man;*
> *Who gives little to take big.*
> *I will not be the mistress of a wife snatcher.*
> *On my knees I plead with you once again*
> *To beg my wicked old granny*
> *Not to pawn me to a lousy miser*
> *The bicycle repairer is a lousy miser.*

The chorus followed with another song:

> *Brother mechanic, son of Maiyali*
> *It is your white teeth that charms me always,*
> *And your moonshine clothings*
> *As handsome as you are, again*
> *My old granny will not let me wed you*

The songs went on and on. Soon the ceremony was coming to a close. The clouds above were amassing in multitudes and they appeared to be overflowing the bank of the vast space and drowning the stars. The moon emerged and sank intermittently as the clouds continued to run over it like a dissipating crowd. Perhaps it would rain. It was everyone's wish that rain should fall. It would be a soothing relief for a night well spent. To Hamida and Ansi it was a beautiful night.

That night both of them stayed awake. Ansi was uncomfortable with the increasing intimacy between him and Hamida. The girl possessed some mystic treasures he found himself seeking to discover. She obviously possessed some charm and he had been bewitched by Hamida's charm.

Hamida too was aware of the growing intimacy between her and

Ansi but she was not alarmed. She had left everything to God and considered everything from the point of view of predestination. What will be will be and what we want may be if we remain persevering and unwavering in faith and hope, she decided.

The wind started with a shrieking noise, then hurling itself at the door with a bang. It cried and howled like an angry monster, tearing through the trees and collided with the window sill. It rushed through various entrances, scattering calendars and paintings on the walls. The gale continued to rage while some strange forces appeared to stem down the rain. It was about the beginning of the rainy season. The rain was coming early this time.

Dust littered doorways and verandahs. A tree fell amidst the uproar of thunder. Somewhere in the distance, an irate dog was howling. Peace was disturbed for over a quarter of an hour while ominous darkness enveloped the atmosphere. Then the rain came with a pent-up rage, cascading heavily like horse hoofs on the roof tops before settling down to a rhythmic drizzling. The rain beat then became music.

Where Hamida slept, she felt some exhilaration running through her. She felt inner peace and satisfaction. Was it the rain or the beautiful dance they just witnessed? Or was it meeting with Ansi? Hamida was not sure of what exactly was responsible for the spiritual elation she felt. But she was aware of the strange mirth within her whenever she was in the company of Ansi. Was this love? Hamida soon drifted into a dreamless sleep. By the time she woke up in the morning she felt whole and fulfilled. The visit to Dakata perhaps might signal the beginning of a new dream.

The Hunter's Whistle

Lara had been standing under the tree for about a quarter of an hour waiting for a vehicle that would take her to the village. She had just stepped down from the luxurious bus that brought her from the Central City. The shade provided by the tree made the environment tolerable despite its unkempt nature. Where she stood was the rendezvous of farmers who came to Efomo to market their farm produce. Peels of yams, leaves of solid pap, cobs of corn and the left-over of devoured delicacies littered the environment. Lara had to clear off some of the wastes so as to reduce the stench.

Efomo was a sharp contrast to where Lara was coming from. It was ironical that the over 700 km double-lane expressway from the Central City could not be extended to this small village that had produced several prominent statesmen and technocrats. The road leading to Efomo was a brown, dust-emitting unhewn path. That was why most vehicles avoided the road. Not more than three vehicular traffic was recorded on the road per day with the most frequent of them being a 504 pick up van owned by a cocoa merchant.

One had to time a visit to Efomo so as not to be stranded. On a market day, vehicles frequented the village. Market women came enmasse and the whole atmosphere would be charged with an air of commerce. Lara had miscalculated by choosing a non-market day to travel. She could not have known. She had been away from the village for long since she gained admission to the National University, Central City.

She looked at her wristwatch. It had stopped at 9.27 a.m. She shook it and it began to work again. The wrist-watch was due for repair. If she had known she would have taken care of it before leaving. Lara was carried away by watching two swirling kites in the sky. They swam in the open sea of the sky. There must be a bonfire somewhere, she thought, and strained her nose to catch the pungent smell of bush burning. She could smell life; pristine village life distinct from the poisonous fume of the automobiles in the cities. She began to reflect on the simple agrarian lifestyle of her people.

Lara was hungry and tired. She picked the left-over of the biscuit she bought at Zuru and began to munch it. She prayed a vehicle should come soon. She had waited for 24 minutes already.

She had been away from the village for two years and had come now to seek sanctuary among her people and also to mend her mutilated heart. She had received bruises from a love turned sour. A retreat to the village would nurse her back to life, she thought.

Remembering James Mantu brought the pain back. Immediately she lost interest in the biscuit she had been munching and sadness suffused her entire body like the evil wind that carried fever. The problem was not with James Mantu at all but with her parents who had constituted a stumbling block to the materialisation of their love affair.

Lara remembered the incident at the dining table that evening. They were having their supper. She had been apprehensive since she came to join the family at the table because of the choleric way her father had been staring at her.

"See your daughter now!" her father had shouted. Lara, in annoyance, had told him she was old enough to keep company when he asked about the identity of the man who came in with her a few moments ago.

"I tell you this girl has been going about doing some immoral acts. No one should bring an unwanted pregnancy to this house, you hear me?" he warned.

"This is unfair Baba Gbenga. Why must you accuse your daughter unjustly like that? Have you seen her with anyone before?" her mother had countered.

"So you are her accomplice in this matter? Ask her. Ask your daughter how many men have been sleeping with her. I have told her no one should bring an unwanted pregnancy into this house."

"Ah," the mother exclaimed.

"Mustn't I enjoy some privacy as a woman? Why must daddy pry into my life everytime?" Lara shouted and made to dash away from the dining table. In a fit of anger he threw a piece of yam which hit her on the forehead.

Lara cried. Her mother quickly rushed at her and took her to the kitchen to clean her face with water. She returned, panting in fury. "You this stupid man. What's wrong with you sef? Will you marry your daughter? Sometimes I think you dey craze sef," Lara's mother ranted.

Threatening, Lara's father warned her, "I have told you. The day she brings an unwanted pregnancy here, both of you must go."

Lara's mother hissed at him and stormed into the bedroom to meet her daughter. The old man sat down heavily still panting from his infuriated mood. He looked for a stick of cigarette, struck a match and lit it. He was shaking both his head and legs at the same time.

"I know all along she would become a loose girl. Such insolence and disobedience from so small a girl. Well that's what the university is breeding these days."

Inside the bedroom mother and daughter were talking. Lara's mother began in a motherly tone. "You know how serious your father is about discipline yet you dared to flout his rules. Would you make your father angry just for the fun of it?"

"Let him eat his discipline mama. He doesn't care about me so, I don't want to talk about him at all," she replied in anger.

"God forbid that you should speak about your father in such a tone. It is a taboo. Don't be a bad girl Lara, it's bad," her mother countered.

Lara was silent and sullen. Both she and her mother were looking at each other without communicating. It was her mother that first broke the silence again.

"You are a grown-up Lara. You have just a year to finish the university. By the time you finish you should be thinking of getting married. Now who is the man in your mind?" she asked.

"It's someone you know," she replied.

"Who is it?"

"James Mantu, the Police ASP."

"Ah!" the mother exclaimed. "You know the consequence of this my daughter. You know your father's view about ethnicity and religion. I will advise you to reconsider this. Hm ... this is serious."

"Mama, this is a matter of love. It has nothing to do with tribe or religion. James Mantu is my man."

"You know your father will never concede to this Lara. Please reconsider it," her mother advised.

"There is no problem mama. Just talk to daddy and if he refuses it's my marriage, not someone else's. Let me bear my cross by myself."

"Do you think his parents would even accept you into their family? You are a stranger to them Lara. You will be safe only among your people," her mother retorted.

"Okay, I have heard you mama. Let me have some sleep now.

We'll talk again tomorrow. But mama if you want my peace and happiness it's James Mantu or no one else," she concluded.

"Alright, we shall talk. We shall talk tomorrow. But you must apologise to your father in the morning."

That was how they ended the discussion.

In the morning the matter got worse. Lara's father would hear nothing of James Mantu or any policeman for that matter marrying his daughter. He forbade Lara from receiving any male visitor. When things became too tough for Lara, she decided to take a break by coming to Efomo.

The hooting horn of a car raised her hope. She prayed fervently that the car should stop for her. Immediately she saw the green coloured Volkswagen car, she knew the occupant was the principal of the only high school in the village. The principal had a nasty habit of playing music with the horn of the car whenever he was driving. This act normally would send truant schoolboys into hiding whenever he was coming. Lara did not like the principal but she needed transport badly. The car came to a halt where she waited. Mr. Balogun never lost sight of a woman. He was already congratulating himself on the opportunity of making a new acquaintance.

"Oh God of mercy," he exclaimed. "So, it's you Lara!" He was excited, his eyes playing some puzzling game inside his old spectacle.

"Welcome sir," Lara greeted her old master. Most educated people in Efomo passed through the high school and must have been taught by Mr. Balogun.

"Have you been standing for long?" he asked full of concern. Among Efomo girls, he respected Lara because of her brilliance and beauty.

"About an hour ago," replied the lady.

"Incredible," shouted the principal. "Oh no, sorry. Hope you are not too tired?" he asked.

"Not at all sir," she replied still feeling the yawning gap that existed between a teacher and his pupil. Lara never trusted the principal. He had his eyes on anything beautiful and until he satisfied his lust, he never gave up easily. He was a leech, a parasite.

They were soon driving along the brown lane that criss-crossed through the bush. Their only company on the road were the birds and rodents that dashed across the road from time to time. Once they saw a monkey. They almost crushed a squirrel that sprinted across their path.

"How is the university?" her host asked.

"Fine sir. It's a beautiful place. A real place to be."

"Hmm ... I'll like to be there sometimes. I'll come to Central City some day."

"It's a nice place to visit."

"Hmm ... That's right."

They were now entering the deserted village. It was normal to find the village desolate on a non-market day. Most able-bodied men would have gone to the farm, and the children would be at school. Mr Balogun's car was the only sign of existence that disturbed the stillness of the late morning air.

The principal dropped her in front of their compound promising to check her in the evening. The lady looked around but could not find anybody. Where could Uncle Ajo have gone? Was he well enough to resume farming? She learnt he had fallen down from a tree about two months ago and had broken a leg. Lara decided to stroll to her grandmother's shed. Her shoes were giving her a problem, as she could not balance her gait on the undulating terrain. She should have worn flat shoes.

Lara passed by the local tap and was surprised to see it flowing ceaselessly. She made an unsuccessful attempt to stop it. She was still struggling with it when a man passed by and told her it had been like that for one week. It had been spoiled by some urchins who turned it into a plaything. It might have to continue like this for another week.

She continued till she got to the famous cashew tree. The tree had been cut. She was depressed with the spectacle. She saw the cutting of the tree as the destruction of a childhood dream. She used to follow boys and girls to pick cashew here. The boys used to come with catapults while the girls picked the cashew that fell from each sling. A stop was put to that when the stone from a teenager's catapult hit an old woman in the face. From then on it was an offence to be found near the tree.

Lara's grandma was in her late eighties. She had a pair of glasses on to aid her eyesight. Lara often wondered how she managed to live on those empty bottles, tins and herbs which she sold. Most of these were gifts from people and wastes thrown on the streets. Somehow her customers find some use in the things she displayed for sale.

"Afternoon ma," Lara greeted the absent-minded woman who was startled. At once she broke into a song praising her family tree and lineage.

"My right eye had been quivering since morning. When it does like that I always know that something good is on the way. How are you my daughter?" she greeted.

"Fine mama," replied the young lady, kneeling as required by tradition. She put down her bag, grateful that she met her grandma at the shed.

The old woman inquired about everybody, her parents and the other children. She was happy to see her grand-daughter.

* * * * * * *

When everyone else had left for the farm in the morning, Lara decided to take a stroll to the countryside. She had declined following Uncle Ajo to the farm today. Her uncle had plantations of cocoa, coffee and rubber. He was also the village chairman of the Farmers Cooperative Union.

Outside in the streets, late starters were seen hurrying to their farm site. Lara walked on slowly enjoying the fresh breeze. She came across a pregnant goat being pursued by an irate dog. The pregnant goat was running with difficulty. She was affected. Lara took a stone and hauled it at the dog. The dog increased its speed. She ran after the beasts until the dog gave up and took another path. Lara's chest burned for want of air.

She continued her walk till she got to the house of the headhunter. It was an old dilapidated building which had been abandoned since the mysterious death of the owner. The headhunter was a reserved personality who hardly spoke until he was drunk. Then, he would sing a riotous tune and fire his dane gun indiscriminately. Whenever he was in a foul mood he would yell obscenities at his imaginary enemies whom he alleged had been collaborating with his rivals to ruin his life.

Whenever he was in his choleric mood the villagers would run in and bolt their doors. No one had been able to check him, not even the *Baale* of Efomo. That was some years ago. The villagers had woken up one morning to find the headhunter lying in a pool of his own blood. He had bled to death. Some said he had been poisoned. The mystery surrounding his death was not unravelled until his rival on the *Oloriode* title himself disappeared. That was when the villagers became convinced that there had been a *juju* war.

Lara took the footpath that led to Efomo High School, her alma mater. It was a season of the green grasshopper. The insects flew from leaf to leaf. They formed a canopy of green foliage. Lara was tempted to start catching them. The green grasshoppers when fried served as a rich snack among the villagers. When taken with *gari* in the afternoon it was a delightful lunch. The bush smelled of the swarm of insects.

Lara marvelled at the pristine village life. There was a season for everything. It would soon be season for the new yam and the garden egg, which often coincided with the season of the mushroom. During the *olu* season the villagers hardly bother about meat. A lunch or supper of pounded yam and stew made with melon and mushroom was very refreshing.

She soon got to the high school. The students were on vacation so the compound was desolate. She took her seat on a painted stone facing the assembly ground. As she sat she remembered Mr. Balogun, the loquacious principal. He had visited her the night before talking about love. Lara was amused. She had simply dismissed the idea by telling him she had come to the village to tell her grandmother she was bringing her fiance home for introduction. That settled it. The principal left with disappointment boldly written on his face.

That experience made the young lady to broach the matter with her grandmother. She told the old woman about how her parents had disapproved of James Mantu.

The old woman sighed. "Where is this man from? She asked.

"He is from Gboko and he is a policeman," she replied.

"Police!" she exclaimed and broke into a song. *"Omo olopa e somo re. Bi o jo kumo a jo kondo."*

Lara was angry at her grandma. The woman quickly sensed her anger and pacified her.

"My daughter, I can see you are angry. Don't mind me. I just remember what our people used to say about the child of a policeman. They say if a policeman's son does not resemble a club he'll resemble a cudgel. Well, my daughter, the world is now a strange world. Your parents are simply worried for your future."

"Mama, James Mantu is very nice. He's prepared to do anything for me."

"Hm ... " the old woman sighed again. "I understand a mind in love listens to no excuse. I understand you perfectly. Like I said the world has changed. Things are no longer the same." Grandma Tobe took her snuffbox and inhaled some quantity. She sneezed and spots of tears became noticeable in her eyes. She cleaned her eyes with the edge of her wrapper.

"In those days" she began, "when a king wanted a wife for himself or his prince and he could not find a suitable girl around, he would send envoys to neighbouring villages in search of a beautiful maid. That was the practice in the past but the world has grown so large now and people have become very different. The world today is full of evil men and women. That's the fear of most parents. Do you remember Mosun?"

"Yes, daughter of Baba Ishola," replied Lara

"Do you remember what her husband did to her?"

"No."

"Now listen."

"I'm all ears mama."

"When Mosun brought that Igbako man as her husband, my husband of blessed memory and all of us were against the union. But Mosun was adamant. We all left her as it is said that a dog that must go astray will not hear the whistle of the hunter. Mosun followed the man to Igbako. It was not until the birth of her third child that a problem set in. The man left home one day and has never been seen again. What we hear are stories that the man had settled somewhere in Iboland and had taken another wife. Mosun is alone with the children now with no helper. She has even refused to remarry. She is still waiting for the man."

"The man is a very wicked man. He deserves nothing but death," Lara spoke with bitterness in her voice. She was afraid. Why were there so many negative stories told whenever someone contemplated marriage?

"Take time to study your man. The world is a strange place. If you look well enough you'll never fall into deceit," Grandma Tobe advised.

Lara was confused. "But James Mantu is so nice. He has never made me unhappy," she ranted.

"I do not want to discourage you my daughter. As it is said. Look right and left before you cross the road. Search your mind, my daughter you'll find the way."

Arrow of Fate

Rafia had been sick for over a week. The family could not afford the exorbitant bill at the hospital, so she was kept indoor. Instead a nurse in the local hospital had been attending to her. She was a very strong woman. Rafia had never been known to have been sick for that long. Her husband, Karu, and his younger brother, Fatahu were in the room attending to her. Fatahu was talking to his brother about the condition of the sick woman.

"Has she taken her drugs this morning?" Fatahu asked.

"No she has not taken anything, even the pap we gave her, she vomited it," replied Karu.

"Do we take her to the hospital then since she has not improved? I'm afraid her condition may deteriorate if we continue to keep her here," canvassed Fatahu.

Karu sighed deeply. He looked worried. Rafia had not even opened her eyes once since morning. Karu felt a pang of guilt. He felt a sense of shame for not being able to take care of the sick woman who was the mother of his three children. Since his retirement as a gateman at the ministry over two years ago life had been unbearable. His wife who had been supplementing the family's income through her petty trading had been lying critically ill for over a week.

"My dear brother, money is the problem, not that one does not know what to do," stated the husband.

"In that case let's send for Nurse Fati," suggested Fatahu.

"Yes let's send for her whatever she says."

Karu moved his chair close to the bed. He felt her hands. Her palms seemed very cold. Fatahu joined him and felt her palms too.

Karu spoke to her. "Rafia open your eyes, and talk to me. Do you feel any pain? Why won't you take your drugs? For God sake have mercy on us and respond to treatment," he pleaded.

The woman neither opened her eyes nor spoke. He was afraid. He told Fatahu to go and fetch Liman Soule. He needed to confide in someone on the next line of action. Perhaps help could come from the community people. For some years now life had been a bundle of woes for everybody.

"How is she now?" Liman Soule asked when he came in.

"She is cold all over. Her breathing appears irregular. She gasps. Ha, what will happen now?" Karu lamented.

The sick woman half-opened her eyes, attempted to speak, made a final jerky movement and laid still. Silence like an ominous wind descended on the small room. Everyone inside felt a cold sensation in their spines.

"Inna lilahi wahinna ilaei rajihun," whispered Liman Soule. "Rafia has gone to join the ancestors. Farewell, good woman. Take heart Karu," he consoled. "The Lord gives and he takes."

Bracing himself up for the misfortune, Karu grinned and hardened his face. He knew very soon the house would become filled with people. Within minutes there was wailing from the backyard and people began to troop into the compound. They covered the deceased and hurried out to go and prepare the burial ground. He quickly sent Rafia's first born, Tadare, to Padongari to go and brief his in-laws.

The young boy knew the enormity of his assignment. He must pull himself together to be able to deliver the message. He passed through the wailing women, some of whom tried to pull him and he burst into a fresh tide of tears. He hurried out of the compound. He was soon in the market place where voices babbled in the haggling trade. "The world is a market place," he echoed a statement by Liman Soule. He began to think of his mother. In his young mind, he pictured his mother climbing the layers of the cloud, trying to reach the heavens gate before nightfall.

Tadare joined a bus that would take him to Padongari. Nights of insomnia soon began to take grip on him. He had been assigned the task of staying by the dead woman's bedside in case she woke up by midnight. He drifted into a fitful sleep. He woke with a start not quite 15 minutes later. The apparition of his mother appeared floating before him. It was so real as if she had not died. Tadare was afraid. He decided he would not sleep again.

He came down at the bus-stop and started walking down the footpath. He was lucky to meet his grandfather who was cutting some peels from trees to make the local concoction for fever.

He greeted the old man who did not seem to have any premonition of bad news coming.

"You are welcome my son. How is your mother and everybody?" he asked.

The young boy was silent. Instead of talking, tears flowed from his eyes.

"What is the problem? Is everyone alright? Come tell me everything, what could have gone wrong?" shouted the old man who was visibly agitated.

"It is mother. She is … ," stammered the lad. "What is it? What has happened to her? Is she sick?" he asked, his breathing becoming impaired.

"No," said the boy.

The old man shook him. "Then, what has happened? Tell me now."

The boy broke down, sobbing uncontrollably. "Mother is dead," he cried.

Something seemed to have somersaulted in Grandpa Lare's heart. He gripped the boy by the shoulder. The boy wept aloud.

The old man paced about the small hut. In the distance, there were men and women at work in the field. They did not seem to know what was going on. He began to soliloquise. "So, Rafia is gone! Ha, my child! What have I done to deserve this?" He shook his head. "The Lord gives and He takes. My heart bleeds in anguish but what can I do? There is no shield strong enough to stand the arrow of fate. We all must answer the call one day."

He sighed. "Go now, but do not tell anyone. I will come down first to see the situation of things, "he instructed the boy.

The boy wiped his face and began to saunter towards the road again.

The old man resumed his soliloquy.

"The Lord is indeed unpredictable. Who could have thought Rafia would die now. She is my only child. Why did God take away my light so soon? Who will comfort me in my old age now? I will go there now. I must see my daughter's remains before they commit her to mother earth. Rafia my child. Sleep well. May Ya'Allah bless your soul. Great Umu Sara, my wife. We'll all meet soon." The old man sang a sorrowful dirge, which the birds of the trees seemed to echo as they cooed and cooed.

Inside the small room where the corpse laid, the women were still mourning. They spoke about the dead. Rafia was the love of all.

"Have they sent for her people? They cannot bury her until her parents come," remarked Umu Rafa.

"Her son had been sent to Padongari. They expect her old man any moment from now. It is a pity. The good ones don't last. It's quite unbelievable that such a good woman should just die like that," contributed Umu Safu.

"Rafia was a nice woman, very friendly to everyone. She is destined for al-janah," stated Adia, her trader colleague.

They had sat there waiting for those who will bathe the corpse. The grave diggers had completed their task. Someone went for the white cloth and the scent. Everyone had kept quite, each submerged by a personal grief. It was Umu Rafa who first noticed the movement on the bed.

"She moves. The dead moves," the woman shouted and there was commotion in the room. The men, including Liman Soule ran to the room.

"Water!" cried the figure on the bed.

"God is great, Ya'Allah is a true God. Someone, bring water quick," shouted Karu. He held Rafia's hand. It was becoming warm. The neighbours who had run away quickly converged again. Someone brought water in a cup. He fed her with it. She coughed, and tried to speak, coughed again, till Karu restrained her.

"How are you now?" asked Liman Soule.

"I feel very light. I feel like I am floating in the air," she replied, her voice faint but clear like that of a new born.

"Ah, can this be real?" exclaimed Adia.

"Do you feel alright, no pain?" asked Karu with concern very palpable in his voice.

"I'm perfectly alright. I have gone on a journey, a great journey. Someone is here let me see his face," she demanded.

Grandpa Lare who appeared confused came in. He rushed at his daughter when he saw her.

"Rafia my child, what has happened to you. Didn't they say my daughter has passed on. I did well by not telling anyone. I had my doubts." The old man wept and clung to the bosom of the revived woman.

"I saw your father, Haileru and he sent me with a message for you Papa," said the strange woman.

Grandpa Lare was not sure of what he heard Rafia said. "You saw who?" he asked.

"I saw Haileru your father, my own grandfather."

The old man knew something was amiss. What sort of response was he supposed to give to that statement?

There was absolute silence in the room. Many had heard of the dead coming back to life but it was the first time anyone would see it in reality. They all stared at the woman in disbelief.

"I saw Haileru, the brave one," repeated the woman. "He took me round the beautiful scenery of paradise. I saw the magnificent brooks and fountain. They flow between the lustral garden, deep green and ravishing in their celestial adornment. He took me round the beautiful chalets of paradise surrounded by beautiful multi-coloured birds. Their music was enchanting and soul-elevating. Ya'Allah is truly a great one."

The people who had gathered exclaimed, "Ya'Allah is truly great."

"I was escorted by a retinue of angels in white robes. I felt like a queen. Truly I was dressed like a queen. I did not want to leave again. I wished to stay on but Haileru insisted I must return. I needed to pass on the message of bliss before I return. Who does an atom weight of good will see it. Who does an atom weight of evil will see it too. Ya'Allah is truly a just God."

"Praise be to Ya'Allah the great one," the people chorused.

"Where is Karu, my husband?" the woman asked. Karu who had been standing, watching the scene without knowing what to do announced his presence. He was beginning to fear whether the happiness he had felt with the resuscitation of his wife could really last.

"Come near me," the woman directed Karu. "I want to pray for you," she stated. Everyone looked surprised.

"I'm no longer an ordinary person," she resumed. "I have embarked on a great journey which only the anointed of Ya'Allah have undertaken. You will never know sadness as you've been clothed in the garb of Mahfouz. Take care and don't waver."

The people who had waited sighed. Tadare had been sobbing in a corner. The young boy could not understand the transformation his mother had been going through. The woman continued talking. She was the only one talking in the room.

"I'm one of the daughters of light. I bring light to this dark plain. I'm a progeny of the one who brought light to this community. No one should grieve on account of me."

Tadare cried more. Outside a woman began another round of wailing. Liman Soule and Karu looked at each other. Something must be done. They started dispersing the people. The woman must be allowed to rest.

"Look she has gone to sleep," Liman Soule tried to pacify the angry people. "Let her have some sleep. Karu, see to it that no one disturbs her. Let someone prepare a very hot pap for her, look for milk and some dates. Let her feed on light food till she is strong enough," advised Liman Soule.

Karu thanked his friend. "Don't be long Liman Soule. You're very kind. Please don't be far from us."

Grandpa Lare called Karu after and spoke about organising prayers for Rafia or taking her to the hospital. She needed some special care as things were with her.

As if listening to them, Rafia called from the bed, "I need some water." They brought her food which she declined. "I have just repeated the trip," she remarked. Tadare began crying again and he was scolded by the men.

The woman resumed. "Why do you cry so, my son? I forbade all of you to cry. I'm beyond mortal care now. I live in the midst of the ancient and holy people. I shall be their link with you all. Now everyone should go to sleep."

"It is still daytime, Rafia, can't you see?" remarked Karu.

"I want to sleep now. I need some peace," insisted the woman.

They started going out but halted their steps when they heard her coughing.

"Water," cried the woman. Tadare ran to bring the water. Karu tried to feed her with it. She half-opened her mouth, gave a violent jerk and the cup fell on the bed.

Tadare cried. "Mama, please don't leave us. Please!"

Grandpa Lare shrugged his shoulder in a sign accepting defeat. "This looks like the end," he whispered. "I shall not weep. No, I won't."

There was wailing. The women wailed. Gradually, consciousness took its leave of her till she went limp. There was loud wailing. Someone had run to call Liman Soule. They all resolved that the dead had merely returned to clear some unfinished business.

After the interment, Liman Soule spoke to the people. "What has happened here is not a common occurrence. Let us learn from it. In everything that happens in life, there is a message for humanity. No one should grieve. We should rather reflect and prepare for our own end. Ya'Allah is the only true God."

It was the muezzin's call to prayer that dispersed the crowd. Rafia's story became a myth and the story was taken from clan to clan and beyond.

www.ingramcontent.com/pod-product-compliance
Lightning Source LLC
Chambersburg PA
CBHW070934160426
43193CB00011B/1681